A Thousand Miles
from Wall Street

A Thousand Miles from Wall Street

Tony Gray's
Commonsense Guide to
Picking Stocks

Tony Gray
Kurt Greenbaum

MACMILLAN • USA

MACMILLAN
A Prentice Hall Macmillan Company
15 Columbus Circle
New York, NY 10023

Library of Congress Cataloging-in-Publication Data

Gray, Tony (Anthony R.)
    A thousand miles from Wall Street : Tony Gray's commonsense guide to picking stocks.
       p.   cm.
    Includes index.
    ISBN 0-02-545167-7
      1. Securities—United States—Handbooks, manuals, etc.   2. Stock
-exchange—United States—Handbooks, manuals, etc.   I. Title.
    II. Title: Commonsense guide to picking stocks.
    HG4921.G715   1995
    332.63'22—dc20   95-3843   CIP

10 9 8 7 6 5 4 3 2 1
Printed in the United States of America

To my wife, Lacey, and children, Ashley and Kipp.
While they don't pick any stocks for me,
when my picks go down,
they make coming home
a lot more enjoyable.
A.R.G.

To Janis, for never doubting I could do it,
and to Sarah, for sharing her first three years with it.
K.G.

ACKNOWLEDGMENTS

What this lacks in verbosity, we hope it makes up for in sincerity. From Tony, thanks go to Richard F. Hokenson, chief economist for demographics at Donaldson, Lufkin & Jenrette for his assistance and insight. From Kurt, thanks go out to Jeffrey Taylor, whose recommendation made it possible for him to be involved in this project at the start; Edward Novak for bringing him along; Rick Wolff, who whipped the early drafts into shape; Eric Wechter, who sheperded it through production with a perfect balance of care and haste; and especially to Emily Heckman, who resuscitated the project beautifully after the machinations of Corporate America tried to do it in.

CONTENTS

A Thousand Miles
from Wall Street

1

Introduction

The summer closeout sales had begun, and I was ready to spruce up my wardrobe a bit, so I flew into Marshall's at the opening bell on the first day of the sale. I left with a suit, four dress shirts, four golf shirts, four pairs of socks, a windbreaker and a couple of other small accessories. I was practically giddy when I got home, begging my family to guess how much I had spent on this cornucopia of clothing.

Well, the giddiness obviously showed, and my family was well aware that I am basically the cheapest person they knew in the world. They lowballed their guess beyond all recognition: $150. Absurd! Who could walk away from a store with all that clothing for $150?

When I got back to work on Monday morning, I offered my colleagues the same quiz. Unfortunately, they also knew my reputation and came in with another unrealistically low answer. Everyone must have thought it the most ridiculous answer they could muster up. Surely, no one could buy that much for that little. Well, they were right. I got it all for $85.

I liked the suit, but my wife insists I overpaid. Everyone's a critic.

It's a story I love to tell because it's a good example of how I do business. The clothes I bought were the same as they were three months earlier—everything but the price tag—and I didn't want the clothes badly enough to spend what Marshall's was asking for them in the first place. That's really the key, isn't it? You don't want it badly enough to pay full price. Put it another way: You're willing to walk away if the deal doesn't suit you. But, when the sale started and the merchandise went out, I was ready.

See, I like to find a bargain, just like you and everyone else you know. I like to find a $185 suit, which I actually did, but I only want to spend $65 for it—which I also did. I like to do the same thing in the stock market. So would you.

I manage $4 billion in a group of pooled pension funds and mutual funds that owns shares in more than a hundred different companies.

While some investors tell you to catch the latest technology wave and ride it to riches, I like to own the stocks everyone else owns. I want companies that make stuff you and I have heard of, products and services we understand: soup, medicine, clothing. I hate computers; their technology changes too fast, and I don't understand them, so why should I invest in them? I don't even like to use them. Besides, I don't make any money in technology stocks. I have followed high-tech stocks for 27 years and don't know them now any better than I did when I started. Mayonnaise, I understand. Retailing, I know. Medicine, I understand. Besides, I get a kick out of talking to a cardiologist about the latest heart drug. I know something about it because I own stock in the company that makes it.

While some investors tell you to grab hold of a stock and hang on for the long ride, I disagree. Everything in my portfolio is for sale if the price is right. I like to keep my holdings fresh. My portfolio turns over completely every year. I'm not afraid to hang on to a stock if I think it's cheap and will continue to be a moneymaker. I'm not afraid to get rid of it if it's not. The worst thing you can have is an old stock that hasn't worked. It might have been a mistake to buy it in the first place, but it's a bigger mistake to continue holding it if the potential is not there.

I have no heroes in this business. People get misled too often by "professionals." They get bad advice once and sour on the stock market forever. I have not made those mistakes. I have an investment philosophy—a sound one. It has worked for me my entire professional life. I won't tell you mine is right for you. In this book I will tell you about my philosophy and my methodology. I will tell you why it has worked. I will even tell you how you could adapt it to your own needs. But I won't tell you to use it. That's up to you.

If I had to sum it up in a phrase, it would be "reality versus perception." I buy stock in companies with strong growth potential, good products or an improving outlook. But I only want to buy them cheap. Stock prices only go down when someone, for some reason, doesn't like the stock and sells it. So when someone else perceives a stock as damaged goods, that could be the time to strike. It's a little like the clothes at Marshall's; nothing was wrong with them after the prices were slashed, although some fashion snobs might disagree.

Every stock I buy (or anybody buys) is someone else's castoff. But I expect these frogs to become princes while I own them. I make my living balancing the reality of a company's prospects against the perception of other investors. When reality outdistances perception, I come out a winner.

The trick, of course, is knowing when the reality and the perception part company.

When a broker offered 200,000 shares of Procter & Gamble for sale in late November 1991, I didn't wait around wondering if people had stopped brushing their teeth with Crest toothpaste or washing their laundry with Tide detergent. The perception: Something is wrong with Procter & Gamble because it is falling down the tubes along with the market, which was also falling that day. The reality: Procter & Gamble is a strong company reacting to a glitch in the market. I don't always own it, but when the price is right, I wouldn't turn it down. The broker offered it at $80.50 a share. Knowing his client wanted out and thinking that Procter &

Gamble was damaged goods, I offered to pay $79. And I got it.

Not long after that, the stock was selling for $100 a share. If I sold the stock, I'd make a quick $4.2 million—a return of 26.6 percent. And I might just do that. I'll get what I can out of the stock and move on. I've done it before with Procter & Gamble, when it once made up 3 percent of my portfolio. And I'll do it again.

Think of it this way: When you walk into a department store and find a $300 suit on sale for $120, what's the first thing you do? Do you run home and check your closet to see if you have a shirt and tie that will match? Do you check to see if you need that particular color? Of course not! You're already familiar with your wardrobe and know what you need. So you jump in and buy the suit.

It's the same with the Procter & Gamble stock. I have followed the stock for years, and I know what makes it rise and fall. In this case, I knew why the price was down—people just weren't interested in buying that type of stock during that particular period in the economy. So I didn't have to start from scratch and reanalyze the stock. I bellied up to the bar and bought it. If you want to invest in stocks, you need to know how to make a decision. I make 30 different million-dollar decisions every day.

There's another more obvious lesson to that story. Actually, it's more like a reminder of something you already know: If you're not willing to walk away from the negotiations, then you're not really bargaining. Suppose you're in a shop in Mexico, where every price is negotiable. If you and the shopkeeper strike a price while you're still standing in the shop, you probably didn't wait long enough. You must walk out of the store, head down the street and wait for the shopkeeper to chase you with another offer. Then you know you've struck a good price. The idea is the same whether you're talking about stocks on the trading floor or automobiles on the showroom floor. If someone doesn't accept my first offer, I might bid up a little, but I'll never pay more than I think the stock is worth—period.

The second lesson is less obvious.

The fact is, my success depends on the failings of other investors. I can't do my job without them. Unless someone else does something dumb, I won't look smart. Add to that the timidness, disillusionment, overconfidence, impatience, ignorance and stubbornness of other investors, and you practically have the Seven Deadly Sins of the stock market.

I have always wondered, for example, about the guy on the other end of a trade in October 1987 after the market had fallen 500 points in one day, and his 300,000 shares of CPC International had plummeted. As I write this, the market regularly pushes above 3,700, inching toward 4,000. The crash seems almost like ancient history, doesn't it? But two months before the October 19 crash, that packaged food company had been blazing a trail through the market at $56 a share. And just like Procter & Gamble, the crash hadn't stopped people from cooking Knorr soups to eat with the bologna sandwiches that they had made with Hellmann's Real Mayonnaise— products made by CPC. So when the offer came in at $28 a share on a stock perceived to be damaged goods, I said to myself, "They can only fire me once." I bid for it and bought the whole bunch— for $27 a share. Well, you probably wouldn't be reading this book if the stock had not done well. In six weeks, it went up 20 points. By January 1992, it had tripled.

I'm always glad there are dumb people out there. And, I'm not too proud to say, I've been the dumb one often enough to make me humble. You'll see plenty of examples of that too.

I want to invest in strong, high-growth companies, and I want to find their stock at a bargain price. If that stock doesn't start growing faster than the stock market as a whole—and pretty soon—I start to lose interest. It goes on my doggie stock list. We ask our stocks simple questions: What have you done for me lately? And what can I expect in the next six months?

I've been wrong about several stocks. The Home Depot has swept the nation, selling lumber, garden tools, hardware and home fixtures to would-be do-it-yourselfers and sending the competition into the basement. We knew enough to own it at the outset, but we didn't evaluate it correctly as its stock price started the climb. We got out too soon, when we thought the price had gotten too high and perception had exceeded reality. By the time we caught on to the mistake, the price was higher than we wanted to spend. It was a dumb move. Maybe we thought another retailer looked better at the time. For every stock, there is an alternative. You just hope you're right 55 percent of the time. It took years before I found The Home Depot again at a price I wanted to pay.

The fact is, you have the same chance for success as I have. Despite the fact that I have 600 stock analysts from more than a dozen different brokerage firms at my disposal, despite the fact that I can bid down the price of a stock by virtue of my sizable buying power, your chances of succeeding are still just as good as mine. In this business, the person who knows absolutely nothing about the stock market does as well as the Harvard MBA on average—a scary thought for the Harvard MBA, wouldn't you say? Maybe your chances are better. You don't have to report your results to clients or find a buyer when you own a million shares of stock and its price is tumbling.

On the other hand, maybe you've never given a thought to the stock market in the first place. Most people have virtually no investment program. They probably spend more time picking out a set of golf clubs than choosing a stock they want to follow. I can't help you with your golf clubs—I just got back into the game after an 18-year lapse—but I can help you with your investment program. That's what this book is all about. How do I make money in the market? Could you adapt my ideas to your own portfolio? And what does a stock market investor need to keep in mind about the business in general?

The fact is I'm good at my job, and I have a good idea how to make money. I'd better. The pension accounts that invest in my fund, SunBank's Corporate Equity Fund and the two mutual funds I manage, have a lot riding on my success. Before I came to SunBank, the Corporate Equity Fund actually lost money during a six-year period in which the Standard & Poor's 500 stock index doubled.

Since I took over that fund in 1981, my fund has beaten that bell-wether index in every year but two—and it has never had a down year. The pension fund that invested with me at year-end 1980—and kept it there—increased its original investment 1,150 percent. That's 21.5 percent a year, compounded.

So I know what I'm talking about. When I speak to investors, they ask about my favorite stocks, my outlook for the future and my views on government fiscal policy—my philosophy. Maybe you have the same questions. Why does my way work? Would it work for you?

Remember: I have no heroes in this business. There are other institutional investors whom I respect and admire, but none whom I would emulate. You must develop and have confidence in your own abilities. Successful people in this business develop their own style and stick to it—they do not constantly try to emulate other styles. I view myself as being self-taught. You can be too.

2

So, Who Is This Guy Anyway?

If it's not clear already, it will be by the end of this chapter: I look to steal merchandise any chance I get. That goes for any kind of merchandise, stocks or suits. Consider the Great Sneaker Caper.

A few years ago, in an interview for a magazine article, I mentioned that I couldn't bring myself to buy stock in Reebok or Nike, the top-ranked makers of athletic shoes in the world. I explained to the interviewer that I couldn't relate to a company that basically sells gym shoes for $50 to $100 a pop. I never pay more than $10 for a pair of sneakers.

Of course, this comment hit the press, and my colleagues couldn't get enough of it. The razzing began immediately, and the pressure was on the next time I was in the market for gym shoes. But, as with most deals, I knew better than to go shopping for a new pair of $10 gym shoes. You can never find them when you go looking for them. I would browse from time to time, drop into a sporting goods store if it was on my way, scan catalogs. One day, I struck pay dirt. A sporting goods store that was going out of business had a pair of Chuck Taylor Converse All-Stars—once the Cadillac of the sneaker industry—on sale for the ridiculously low price of $7. Okay, they weren't the most up-to-date basketball shoes in the world—big deal. I don't play basketball particularly well anyway. I only needed them to work in the garden.

Here's another example: In January of 1976, during the coldest week of the coldest winter in Cincinnati history, I found myself wandering around a new car lot looking to replace an old, rusting Camaro. The salesmen were no doubt salivating at the sight of anyone on their lot that day. One salesman in particular was probably stunned to find my eyes set on a new Ford Granada that had been wasting away for nearly nine months on the dealer's lot.

He had good reason to be excited.

This particular Granada sedan, the major new family car of the Ford line at the time, was burdened with a three-on-the-floor manual transmission, the sort of transmission no one wanted anymore. In fact, I hadn't seen that kind of transmission since the 1930s. I didn't mind, however, because I've always been a fan of manual transmissions (my current car, a gold, four-year-old Acura sedan, is a manual). All I really needed was basic transportation. Anyway, what would I have done with more horsepower? But at the dealer's asking price (you won't believe it), this car wasn't exactly a bargain. The dealer wanted $4,700. Remember, the year was 1976, and that was not a bargain. I didn't want it that bad.

Of course, the dealer didn't either.

"There are only two people in this city who are going to buy this car," I told him. "I'm one of them, and neither one of us knows the other."

I offered him $3,990 for the car, and I got it. If I hadn't, I would have found another car. And he knew that.

It's the same with the stock market. Just like the clothes at Marshall's, the merchandise is displayed for everyone to see, and the prices are marked. You can sit around, pondering whether to buy that shirt, or you can let someone else yank it out from under your nose. You can buy a piece of a company for the right price, the sale price, but all the pondering must be done ahead of time. You need to do your homework so you're ready to strike when the opportunity comes along.

At the outset I said making money in the stock market is a skill you can teach yourself—but it will only work if you put some time into it. Just like anything else, a good investment program requires a little sweat equity. A house, they say, may be an investment. But nobody would think so if the owners just let the roof mildew and the paint peel. Success in the stock market requires a little sweat equity too. Looking for the deals takes time, just like finding the $10 sneakers. The stock market eats dabblers for lunch—an expensive, extravagant lunch with three martinis and a rich dessert. And the dabblers pick up the check.

I am at the other extreme. Dabblers pay little attention to the task at hand; I pay constant attention. Dabblers only do the job well when the mood hits them and things go well. I must do my job well all the time, and I must do it *better* when things are bad. My job requires me to live, eat and sleep the stock market, watching every blip across the quote machine. Dabblers have no time for practice. I've had plenty of it.

For one thing, I started early. I probably showed my inclination to put my money to work as a kindergartener in my hometown of Omaha, Nebraska, just before the end of World War II. Even then, I cultivated a cheapskate image: Each week I would collect my allowance (a dime a week, plus any other cash I'd earned) take it to school and buy a stamp. That stamp went into a book. By the end of the school year, I had $18.25 worth of stamps, enough to buy a $25 war bond. I bought another after first grade and another after second grade.

That experience is certainly not unique among people of my generation. Lots of kids bought war bonds. Parents and teachers encouraged it at home and at school. They encouraged it because they believed children should learn how to save their money. I have always believed that some people are born with a savings gene and others are born with a spending gene. I doubt any of the former have been born since 1973. We are constantly hearing about how difficult it is for young people today, how the economy has forced couples to work two jobs to support themselves, how their first home is an elusive dream. If more people had the savings gene, we probably wouldn't be hearing these stories. People can't afford to buy a first home because they refuse to save. Years ago, to buy a $25,000 house, you would have been expected to put away $4,000 or $5,000 to do it. Nowadays, people expect to be able to buy a fancier house than the one their parents started with, one that might cost them $150,000, and with the same $5,000. They don't save. They want fancy cars and fancy clothes instead of looking out for their future. Don't blame the economy; blame the individual.

Thankfully, buying war bonds brought out the savings gene in me. I have often wondered where I'd be sitting now if my parents had encouraged me to make a real investment with the money I'd saved. Suppose I could have bought stock in General Motors when I was in kindergarten, just before all the soldiers came home and bought their new cars and their new houses? I would have had a lot more than $75 by the time I started college.

I earned and saved my money any way I could find. As a youngster during World War II, I sold produce from my "victory garden." I shoveled snow; the tab for scooping the wet, heavy stuff for three hours came to about one dollar. I scavenged for lost golf balls when I got a little bit older. With those free supplies and my allowance, I had enough to play about 10 rounds of golf—at $.50 a round—on the public course each year. If I had stuck with golf the way I've stuck with investing, maybe my handicap now would be a little lower. Whenever my birthday or Christmas came along, I would stash away any money I received. My grandparents eventually had to leave notes with the money, demanding that I find a way to spend it.

My grandfather in particular had a keen interest in the stock market. He would meet weekly with a stockbroker who drove from his office in Davenport, Iowa, to my grandfather's house in Iowa City. I lived there as a graduate student at the University of Iowa. I would sit through these meetings, soaking in the discussion and honing my own interest in stocks. My grandfather was 82 at the time, and his eyesight was poor, so I would read the stock quotes from the newspaper to him. I don't recall his being a particularly shrewd investor; it wasn't hard to do well in the prosperity after World War II. He bought the blue-chip stocks of his day, Bethlehem Steel, Rockwell, AT&T. Some of those stocks were great in the '50s and '60s but became doggie stocks in the '70s and '80s. My grandfather was smart enough to get into the stock market when relatively few people were doing it. And he was smart enough to know this: It's never too late. He bought his first stock at age 70. When he died in 1965 at age 85, he was quite well off. All this continued to kindle my interest in the stock market. I didn't wait too long to act on that interest.

I bought my first stock when I was a 19-year-old college student. I plunked down $280 and bought 10 shares of United Fruit, the corporate ancestor of Chiquita Banana. For a while, I strutted around campus, trying to impress my friends with my financial savvy. I'd pick up the paper, check my stock and announce my latest gains to anyone who would listen. My friends were only mildly interested. After all, this was 1959 and I wasn't exactly playing in a rock and roll band.

Six months later, Fidel Castro shut me up in a hurry. When he took over as Cuban premier in February 1959, he seized all the property in the country for himself—including my banana plantations. I considered those plantations to be my property and therefore took it personally when Castro's actions stripped United Fruit of a major asset. Take away a big chunk of a company's assets and what do you suppose happens? Right! The company's stock price dipped to $14 a share—half what I paid for it.

I never said another word to my classmates about my investment. Like all good investors, you never tell anybody when your stocks are down, only when they're up. That is one rule that hasn't changed over the years.

Fortunately, I was distracted by college and did not have time to panic over the thrashing I had taken. I held on to United Fruit for three years, through the rest of undergraduate school and into my first year as a graduate student. As semester break approached,

I intended to sell the stock because it finally returned to the price I had paid for it. But suddenly, just before I made it home for the break, my stock jumped to $31 a share! I sold it. After more than three years of holding this stock, I had made nearly 11 percent.

I had no idea why!

My first foray into the stock market taught me to learn something about whatever I was buying. I had no information at all about United Fruit. All I knew was what ran in the paper every day, that strip of tiny numbers on the stock page. I first bought it because of a recommendation from a stockbroker who was the uncle of a friend, a man I never spoke to from the time I bought it until the time I sold it. I never knew why it went up in the beginning. I could obviously figure out why it went down. But I had no idea why it rallied. I learned a little something with that experience: Every time I bought a stock after that, I knew more than the time before about the process. I knew more about the company and more about why I bought it.

After peeling out of United Fruit, President Kennedy made me look even smarter. I sold out of the stock market shortly before Kennedy confronted U.S. Steel in a nasty face-off over rising steel prices. In April 1962, the major steel producers had announced price increases, and Kennedy lashed back by shifting government orders to rival steel companies and threatening to sue the ones that were raising prices. Kennedy won, but not before the stock market fell 25 percent. U.S. Steel had hit a high of almost $79 a share that year; by the time Kennedy was finished, the company's stock price had fallen to $37.75. And I was free and clear of the bloodshed.

At that point, at the bottom of the market, when everyone expected the debacle with U.S. Steel to spark a recession, I went back into the stock market with more money than before—$1,500 this time. Despite the government's spanking of the steel industry, I bought stock in McLouth Steel, a major supplier to General Motors. That recommendation came from my grandfather's stockbroker. Within six months, the stock had climbed 50 percent. I sold out and put the profits into another auto supplier, Hayes

Industries. That one also rose 50 percent within six months. I have never been out of the stock market since then. Three years later, I decided to make investments my career.

Early success as an investor wasn't the only thing that persuaded me to to make a living at it. In fact, it took me years before I ever made it into this business in the first place. I earned my master's degree in actuarial science, where I learned how to figure the chances of a 50-year-old man dying in a hailstorm—in Iowa—in June. I didn't even know people did what I do now.

My first job was a three-year military stint as a computer programmer and mathematical consultant for the U.S. Public Health Service, the same outfit that told us smoking was bad for our health. I didn't work on that particular project. But I did help answer a couple of other burning questions that, amazingly, someone actually thought needed to be researched. In one case, we researched whether a child will resist temptation more easily if its mother is in the room. Another project involved tickling infants' feet and counting the frequency of their smiles. I plotted the numbers on a graph and made the profound discovery that a child will smile more at the start of the project—as their feet were first tickled—than they did at the end. Do you ever wonder whether there's waste in government? Let me tell you from firsthand experience: yes. I not only saw it, I was part of it.

The money was not great. I took home $376 a month. With half I paid for my food and lodging. The rest I saved, pumping it into the stock market as fast as I could get it.

But I was absolutely terrible as a computer programmer. If I had not been working for the government, I would have been fired. My programs were inelegant. I would use twice as many punch cards as my colleagues to do the same things. Yet someone actually offered me a chance to apply for a career post in the service. I turned them down. In fact, I quickly discovered a job that requires a lot of work on computers isn't right for a guy who doesn't like computers much. I hated my job, I hated to go to work, and I realized that if I didn't have a job I liked, then I wouldn't be any good at it. It's a good lesson for anyone.

My first job out of the service stoked my interest in stocks even more. Lincoln National Life in Fort Wayne, Indiana, had a couple of things going for it. First, the building was air-conditioned. It was a lot easier to put in long hours laboring at the office because my own home was an oven. If nothing else, I could take refuge in the cool building, a huge office building where the management at that time thought nothing of giving me a key to the whole place—after working there only one day. I can remember going to work on weekends, staring down a hallway full of cabinets crammed with research reports. I'd say, "I know there's a good idea in here somewhere. All I have to do is find it." Three hours later, I had my first stock recommendation: Sterling Drug. I used it off and on for the next six years. I made a lot more money off it than did Eastman Kodak, which had the misfortune to buy it many years later.

Another key benefit was the company cafeteria, where I could get three cheap meals a day. But the most important benefit was the company itself. Lincoln National had the greatest commitment to common stocks among any other life insurance company that I had checked out. At the time, most insurance companies put your premiums in what they considered to be less risky investments— bonds and mortgages, for example. The stock market was considered too speculative. Even Lincoln National only had 4 percent of its holdings in the stock market. But it was enough for me.

Working as an analyst, I helped the Lincoln National portfolio manager decide how to invest the company's money. I was the first and only analyst on the staff to work exclusively in stocks. I was extremely lucky to start at this company, where I got a lot more responsibility than anyone else with my level of experience (or lack of experience) should have gotten. As an analyst, I became an expert on certain companies and industries. I knew autos and packaged foods inside and out. I would collect information about a company's earnings compared with competitors', market share and sales. I would look at balance sheets. How much debt does the company have? How much does it pay in dividends? Ultimately, I'd have to decide: Is the company's stock going up or down? Three and a half years later, I was making the princely salary of $13,000 a year when I decided to seek more of a fortune elsewhere. I wanted to put some of my stock market research to use firsthand. I wanted to be a portfolio manager.

Well, things didn't turn out all that well. Between 1969 and 1979, I bounced to five different jobs, each one seemingly worse than the one before. In some cases, the management had promised one job and delivered another. In one case, I was still too wet behind the ears to deal with the stock market decline of the mid-1970s. In my last job, I had virtually nothing to do. By 1979, I was essentially unemployable. I had worked in crummy jobs for crummy companies for so long, I had little to recommend me. Desperate, I read John Malloy's *Dress for Success* and learned that I had at least one strike against me whenever I walked into an interview: I wore light-colored suits. I bought a navy blue pinstriped suit and got job offers the next two times I interviewed. I took the job at SunBank in Orlando.

The new suit notwithstanding, I probably got my first job at SunBank because they didn't have to pay me much. You don't need to pay a man much if he is desperate. The job sounded better than it was: Director of Research. Great title, but at the time, this semistatewide banking operation had only one person doing research on the stock market. I directed myself. Besides, the trust department didn't have an awful lot of assets to manage at the time.

By the end of 1980, I became the portfolio manager (finally!) for the bank's pooled pension fund, a sort of in-house mutual fund for corporate and municipal pensions. When I took it over, it had assets of $1.9 million and ranked in the bottom 2 percent among similar funds for the previous seven years. I am delighted to say that within nine months, it was ranked in the top 1 percent of pension stock funds nationally for the trailing 12-month period. It was all up from that point. At the time of this writing, it is worth $1.5 billion. The price for one unit of my fund has climbed in 13 years from $8.02 to more than $100, an overall growth rate of 21.5 percent a year for the period from 1981 to 1993. Its value has increased almost 1,150 percent, and it has done better than the Standard & Poor's 500-stock index for every year but two. If it weren't successful, this book probably wouldn't be sitting in your lap right now.

That kind of success has changed my job a little too. The more practiced I became as a portfolio manager, the more practice I got to write this book. In 1979, nobody wanted to hear a word I had to say. Nowadays, talking is part of my job. SunBank sends me around the southeastern United States 10 times a year to speak to investor groups, folks who have put their money in mutual funds or pension funds that we manage. They put their money in our hands, and understandably, they want to know a little bit about what we do with it. My deal with SunBank works like this: I'll give the speeches if I don't have to prepare them ahead of time. The last time I brought notes, I walked up to the podium and discovered it was pitch black. I couldn't read a word I wrote.

My audience usually is comprised of people who are somewhere between the dabbler and the professional investor. They recognize that there must be something they can do with their money besides tucking it in the mattress; otherwise, they wouldn't be there in the first place. Their questions are similar from one group to the next; only the answers change as the times change. What's your outlook for the economy? Where's the best place to put my money right now? What do you think of the airline industry? Auto industry? Energy?

As I said, the answers to those questions can change from year to year as well as the answers to a lot of other questions my audiences ask me. But my answer to one question will never change: If you want to know where to put your money *right now,* if you want to get the most bang for your buck, put your money in the stock market. And keep it there.

3

The Old-Fashioned Way

When the track opened for the summer in Omaha, I'd be there with my Daily Racing Form and my dope sheet, handicapping every race, ready to put a few bucks down here or there on the horses that grabbed my attention. I already had years of experience reviewing the performance of the horses. When I was 10, my parents would make their annual pilgrimage to the track only after I'd gone through the Daily Racing Form and given my recommendations.

The first time I went to the track, I was 16 years old, far below the legal age for gambling in the state of Nebraska. Nobody asked for my identification, and I didn't volunteer it for years. I had great luck with the horses. I got to know them. I followed a horse named Butch K. for a while, then I followed his son, Calloway K. I'd split $2 show bets with my mother and more often than not come out ahead. I won my biggest purse on a horse named Tea Napkin— $20 on a $2 show bet. It was an incredible string of good fortune.

By the time the track management first bothered to ask for my ID, I was already 21 years old, and it didn't make any difference— at least, that's what I thought at the time. Some supernatural force somewhere must have decided to have a joke at my expense, how-ever, because on that day, my year-over-year string of good luck evaporated. On that day, I was cursed. I'd put $1 down on a horse to show. I'd lose. I'd put $1 down on the favorite to come in and I'd lose. Seven races later, I had lost every one. I had the Midas touch in reverse: Everything I touched turned to mud. And like the typi-cal gambler, the more I lost, the more I bet. The last two races, I doubled up—and lost again!

For $12, I learned a great lesson. I haven't gambled since.

Oh, I hear what you're saying already: I make my living off the stock market. I place bets every day, but my bookie is standing some-where on the floor of the New York Stock Exchange. I turn to the back of the business section every morning, dope out the horses and put a few dollars on Wal-Mart to win, place or show. Right? That's what you're thinking?

You might see it that way, but I don't. As a 16-year-old school-boy, I thought I had all the information I needed in the *Racing Form*. Study that sucker long and hard. Learn all you can about a horse's past performance on grass, in mud, on a fast track. Who's the jockey? How long is the race? It is hard to resist the analogy to the stock market. How has your stock performed in the past? Who is the jockey—the management? What are the conditions of the track—the economy—today? It's hard to resist, but resist it anyway. Bet-ting on the horses is gambling; betting on the stock market isn't—if you're good at it.

Betting is betting, you say? Maybe, but betting is not necessar-ily gambling. I said I never gamble, but I didn't say I never bet. The key, of course, is knowing when a bet is a gamble. I won't throw down a dollar on a World Series pool or bet on the total number of points in the Super Bowl. The last place you'll ever find me is Las Vegas. For one thing, I'm not exactly a night owl. I go to bed at 10 P.M. For another, I'm reasonably sure I'm going to lose if I gamble in Las Vegas—just as the great majority of people will. For the same reason, I avoid horses, race cars and the state lottery. Those betting institutions wouldn't be around very long if the management expected to give away cash to everyone who walked in the door. I hate putting any money down on my golf game. The most I'm usually willing to wager has nothing to do with currency. If I'm in a sand trap (which I often am), I might bet the princely sum of a golf tee that I can get down in two strokes—but that's mostly a ploy to make me concentrate on the shot and boost my confidence.

I only bet when I'm reasonably sure I'm going to win. Say the odds are 50-50, and I'm 70 percent sure I'm going to win—then I'll put my money where my mouth is.

In my view, that rules out a lot of so-called investments. I could bet on grain futures, but in two weeks the weather could literally wash away my money. I could bet on the price of gold, but it has 14 years of history against it. Gold sold for about twice the price in the early 1980s as it did in the early 1990s. I hear some folks make a killing with antique rocking chairs, priceless works of art by Monet or 175-year-old bottles of Chateau Lafite Rothschild that once sat in Thomas Jefferson's wine cellar. My question is: Where is the market for those things? If you need the money *now*, how do you get it?

This doesn't mean no one is good at investing in gold or futures. It just means I'm not. Don't bet (or invest) unless the odds favor your winning.

You remember the speeches I mentioned before, right? Well in Florida, I often find myself talking to audiences packed with retirees, many of them eager to know how they can stretch a dollar. I have a standard question for them: How many of you think certificates of deposit (CDs) are a good investment? Depending on the economy at the time, maybe half the people in the audience will raise their hands. How many think they're a bad investment? The other half will chuckle, and the hands will go up. My answer to them: You're both wrong. A CD isn't an investment at all. It's a place to put your money while you're waiting to make a decision about where to invest. And if you've had your money there too long, you obviously have trouble making a decision.

Most people don't have any trouble deciding where they should avoid putting their money. That's one reason there isn't a huge market for antique rocking chairs with daily trading prices listed in the newspaper. But there are other more mainstream places to put money, right? How about bonds or real estate? Both are listed in the paper, both draw a huge market—what's wrong with them? Nothing but this: If you look at the figures, then you'll see the stock market has outperformed *every other investment* in almost any period you care to look at since the Great Depression.

Stocks have outperformed bonds, they have outperformed inflation, they have outperformed treasury bills—everything (see Figures 3-1 and 3-2). It makes sense when you consider what the stock market is all about: Investors are buying shares of the American economy. If you have an economy that grows, as it has more often than not, an investment opportunity directly geared to that growth is destined to do well. It is, after all, unusual for the economy to decline.

Top Asset Classes by Decade

The S&P or small company stocks were the number one asset class in every decade since 1926 except one: the 1930s. Shown here is another leading asset and, as a benchmark, inflation.

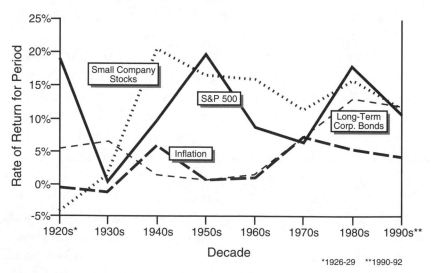

Fig. 3-1
Source: © *Stocks, Bonds, Bills, and Inflation 1993 Yearbook*, Ibbotson Associates, Chicago (annual updates work by Roger B. Ibbotson and REx A. Sinquefield). Used with permission. All rights reserved.

The Dominance of Stocks

From 1926 to 1992, stocks—small or large—have been the leading asset in 42 of those years. Common stocks were the winning asset in 30 out of 67 years, for example. Small company stocks were the leading asset in 12 years.

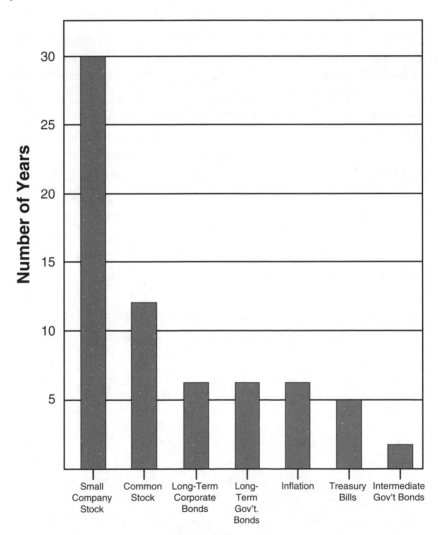

Fig. 3-2
Source: © *Stocks, Bonds, Bills, and Inflation 1993 Yearbook*, Ibbotson Associates, Chicago (annual updates work by Roger B. Ibbotson and REx A. Sinquefield). Used with permission. All rights reserved.

Here's the point: Too many people think investing in the stock market is a gamble. Too risky and no chance to win, they say. If that were true, I wouldn't be doing it. The stock market has plenty of risk; I confront it every day. But you can manage that risk more easily than you can manage the risk at the track. And you know that, on average, anyone who invested in the stock market in the past 10, 20, 30, 40 or 50 years has done a lot better than any other investor.

Besides, your idea of a "safe" investment may not be so safe after all. Inflation rates skyrocketed in the late 1970s and early 1980s. The value of your bonds dropped sharply. Interest rates plummeted from their highs of 16 percent in the 1980s to 6 percent in the 1990s. That means your income from those bonds has dropped along with the interest rates as the money was reinvested. Where were the folks who relied on CDs to supplement their fixed incomes? In the 1970s, they were grousing about how their interest income was being eaten up by rising costs for food and medicine. The 8 percent or 10 percent they were earning couldn't keep pace with inflation. In the 1990s, they were grousing about how their income was being cut in half. Their CDs were earning 6 percent until they rolled them over again. Then they were lucky to get 3 percent.

And they probably thought CDs were "a safe investment."

CDs and Savings Accounts

Years ago, when you walked into a bank with a wheelbarrow full of money, you couldn't expect much help from your banker. There just weren't a lot of investment choices there.

Obviously, there's a savings account. Why bother? Some banks are even charging you a fee for a passbook savings account—those banks that still offer passbook savings accounts, that is. You might not even earn enough interest to cover the fee. As I write this, interest rates are lower than they have been in years. You'd be lucky to get 3 percent on the cash in your savings account. The same is true for a certificate of deposit, a deal in which the bank offers you a guaranteed interest rate over the life of the certificate—six months, a year, maybe two years. The longer you leave it, the higher the interest.

Ten years ago, banks were aggressively marketing CDs as a safe place to keep cash. Interest rates as high as 8, 9, even 10 percent were common. Again, as I write this, banks can't market them with a straight face anymore. The rates are pathetic. I have never owned a certificate of deposit, and I haven't had a savings account for more than 25 years. Why? Because there are a lot of better places to put my money. Banks know that too. That's why so many, like SunBank, are offering mutual funds and other investment opportunities themselves.

My personal savings go in a stock brokerage account. Most of that cash stays in the stock market, invested in a variety of stocks that I monitor as closely as my professional portfolio. Any cash that's not immediately invested automatically goes into a money market fund, offering some interest income while I await my next big buying idea.

Maybe it's a little coldhearted, but I have a hard time working up much sympathy. There is no safe investment—everyone knows that. Invest anyway. Invest in stocks, which I'll show you are the most lucrative place to put your money. A lot of people say they've had a "bad experience" in the stock market. What's a bad experience? They bought a stock and it went down. That's not investing. People tend to get interested in investing when the stock market is going up and everyone is making a lot of money. When things aren't so good, suddenly nobody likes the stock market. Suddenly, it is not acceptable party talk. But investing requires a commitment for the long haul, and I believe everyone should be fully invested all the time.

That means you shouldn't be sitting around with cash under your mattress, in your savings account, in a certificate of deposit or in your wallet. Put it to work. Make money the old-fashioned way: invest it. There are plenty of good reasons. Maybe you're driving a

Toyota Tercel and you're living in a two-bedroom rental apartment. One day, you'd like to be driving a Lexus and living in a four-bedroom house on the waterfront. Astute investing can help you raise your standard of living. Or how about this: Maybe the kids are young now, but you expect they will be going to college when they get older. Preparing for the future is another good reason to invest. One of the best reasons to invest is to protect yourself from the whims of the economy—whims like rising inflation or falling interest rates.

All this is possible, of course, thanks to the greatest invention of the modern age: compound interest. It works in your savings account, but it works a lot faster in the stock market—if you have the patience to let it work for you (see Figure 3-3). If you expect to walk into the stock market one day and walk out the next with a pot of gold, then you'll be taken to the woodshed. You'll get whipped in a hurry. These people have a problem: If someone walked up to them and promised to pay them 10 percent a year on any amount they invested, they'd scoff. They wouldn't be happy. No thank you, they'd say. I can do better. Maybe they can, but why risk it? If you started with $5,000 at age 30 and earned 10 percent a year until you retired 35 years later, then you'd have $160,000. Suddenly, 10 percent looks pretty good—and that assumes you haven't put any more money away for those 35 years. It's a distinct challenge to earn 10 percent a year for any extended period. The average return in the stock market since the Great Depression is 10.3 percent. From 1977 through the 1980s and into the early 1990s, the return has been 16 percent.

Besides, it's a lot of fun. The stock market gives you a great opportunity to learn a little bit about a lot of things. During the 1980s, I owned stock in many of the major drug companies such as Bristol-Myers Squibb, Pfizer and Merck & Co. At parties, I could carry on fascinating conversations with doctors about medicines that weren't even on the market yet. I can debate tobacco liability with 99.9 percent of the people out there because I've spent years investing in Philip Morris. Very early in my career, I remember quoting chapter and verse about the new DC-8 and stretch DC-8 jetliners

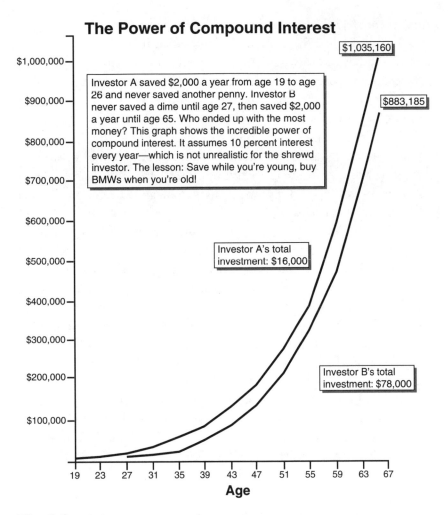

The Power of Compound Interest

$1,000,000 —

$900,000 —

$800,000 —

$700,000 —

$600,000 —

$500,000 —

$400,000 —

$300,000 —

$200,000 —

$100,000 —

Investor A saved $2,000 a year from age 19 to age 26 and never saved another penny. Investor B never saved a dime until age 27, then saved $2,000 a year until age 65. Who ended up with the most money? This graph shows the incredible power of compound interest. It assumes 10 percent interest every year—which is not unrealistic for the shrewd investor. The lesson: Save while you're young, buy BMWs when you're old!

$1,035,160

$883,185

Investor A's total investment: $16,000

Investor B's total investment: $78,000

19 23 27 31 35 39 43 47 51 55 59 63 67

Age

Fig. 3-3

that Douglas Aircraft was building. That's when I realized the stock market is a wonderful place for general knowledge. Everything that happens has something to do with the stock market.

INSIDE LINE

In every corner of every community in the United States, someone is working to build the economy—whether or not they know it. Every farmer, every factory worker, every barber and tailor and newspaper reporter and professional baseball player is contributing to the bottom line of the organization that employs them.

Every few months, government economists gather up numbers to record the pace of thousands of bottom lines all over the country. They crunch those numbers and come up with a figure—the Gross Domestic Product, a profile of the productivity of the nation and its economy. More often than not, that number is bigger than it was the last time the economists did it. The economy wants to grow because the people working in that economy want their paychecks to keep coming, their raises to be good ones and their bonuses to be fat ones.

The stock market is just a way for investors like you and me to cash in on the growth of the economy. If you keep that in mind, then you'll have an easier time in overcoming the thought of risk that goes with any investment. Because the economy wants to grow and the stock market is tied to the success of corporate America, the stock market itself has an upward bias. I'm not suggesting, of course, that there is no risk in stock market investing. All I'm saying is you can define your risk.

With a short-term Treasury bill or a certificate of deposit, you have virtually no risk other than lost opportunity. Your money could be going into more lucractive enterprises. Meanwhile, if you invest in an airline, that's fine too. But you must realize the airline industry is volatile, more risky than other industries you could choose.

Here's the point: You should not dismiss the stock market because it is risky; every investment is risky. You should make a commitment to the stock market as an investor because history is on your side. All you have to do is find and define the right level of risk for you—within the stock market.

Think of it another way: As a kid, you invested in baseball cards because you were interested in baseball, right? But you knew the value of those cards. You knew how many Harry Chiti cards it would take to buy a Wayne Terwilliger. And you knew how unlikely it was that you'd ever see the Great Poobah of baseball cards, the Mickey Mantle rookie card. How about comic books? How many of you are kicking yourself now for letting your father throw away all those issues of *Scrooge McDuck* or *Little Lulu*. How many copies of *Superman* no. 1 went in the trash? You certainly know what you'd do if you found one. Trading cards or comic books were a lot of fun, yet in the back of your mind, there was always an underlying current of thought that went a little like this: What if? The skills you used buying, selling and trading comic books or baseball cards are very similar to the ones you would use to buy, sell and trade stock certificates if the confounded computer age hadn't made them obsolete. Now we have to settle for computerized records of those stocks, but the money is still green.

The point of this whole book is simple: We want to demystify Wall Street a little. We want to show you that half of what you think happens in lower Manhattan is worth ignoring and the other half is stuff you know already—or at least it is stuff you can learn something about. If a kid from Omaha can outperform an army of MBAs from the Big Apple, you can certainly have your share of success.

INSIDE LINE

Don't let your prejudices cloud your judgment when you make investment decisions. I've heard people say they wouldn't invest in a stock like Philip Morris because the company makes cigarettes. I'm opposed to cigarettes myself. I've never smoked a day in my life. But I won't pass up a good opportunity to make money. My job isn't to pass judgment; it's to make money. And that's what Philip Morris has done for years. During the 15 years from 1977 to 1992, the company grew more than 20 percent a year.

The same applies with gambling. As I mentioned, I oppose gambling for a number of reasons. Communities across the nation have been considering whether or not to allow casino gambling. They have opened riverboat casinos on the Mississippi River. They have voted for state lotteries. I think it's all a mistake, sapping our wallets of hard-earned money. But I'm not stupid. A lot of other people don't agree. And I see an investment opportunity. I have a rather large position in International Game Technology, a company that builds slot machines and other casino toys. Do you have any doubts about this gambling craze? The company's earnings grew 45 percent to 50 percent a year since 1988.

We'll see what happens.

Stocks and Bonds and Others

You want to start a business, so you develop an idea for a new product and tell your friends and neighbors about it. You're going to need some cash to get started, to rent that office space, to build the manufacturing equipment and to pay the employees, so you ask around among those friends and neighbors: "Do you want a piece of the action?" They are excited about your product and think it could be a big hit, so they agree to chip in a certain amount of money in exchange for a certificate that entitles them to a share of your business. You've just sold stock in your company.

Now, every cent you earn belongs, in part, to all those friends and neighbors who bought a share (or more) in your company. The desks you bought for the office staff, the inventory in your warehouse all belong to you and to the other shareholders of your company. After awhile, as your product takes off and the world starts to take notice of your company's success, your friends and neighbors start to get offers on their company stock. Someone will offer to pay them more than they paid for a share of your stock. Why? Because they think it is valuable, they expect to reap big gains on your company in the form of dividends and growth as you pay a portion of your earnings back to shareholders. It's not long before your friends and neighbors aren't your only shareholders anymore. Your stock is trading on the market, and folks are buying and selling it at a price that depends on how well your company is doing—or how well they think it is doing.

The value to investors is twofold: How much can they expect to earn from dividends that you pay? And how much can your company's growth continue to push up the price of the stock? Will the price keep going up and up, eventually splitting so, perhaps, shareholders own twice as much stock at half the price?

You own a company, and there are things you need to do: expand, build new equipment, relocate. Who knows? But you're going to need money to do it. So you go out into the world and ask a question all of us have had to ask before: "Can I have a loan?" You ask people to pony up $1,000 each (or more) with the promise that after 30 years, you will pay them back their $1,000 investment plus 8 percent interest each year. "Give me the money now," you say, "and I'll pay you back later on." You've just sold bonds.

Perhaps there are people who buy the bond and wait 30 years for the money that's coming to them. Perhaps, but probably not. Few people sit around waiting 30 years for their investment ship to come in. So they trade the bonds, just as they trade stocks, and the price depends on how valuable they appear to be at the time.

Suppose interest rates have gone up to 12 percent? Suddenly, your bond that pays 8 percent a year is less valuable, and if you sell it, then you will get a lot less than the $1,000 you originally paid for it. Likewise, the opposite is true. If every other bond is paying 6 percent, yours is a bit more valuable because it pays more.

It is 1950 and America still drives on rural routes and back roads. You have a few bucks in your pocket, so you buy a few dozen acres of prime real estate on the outskirts of your town. You don't know what you're going to do with it just yet. Maybe a house, maybe a business, maybe you'll just sell it. Then the interstate highway system comes through, and you discover that you have a hot piece of property. Motel chains want to build on your land, just outside of town. Restaurants and gas stations want to be there. The U.S. government wants to build an interchange on a piece of your land. You've made a mint because your land has suddenly become a heap more valuable. You sell.

As an 8-year-old child, you collected comic books. Each month you went to the dime store for the latest installment of *Little Lulu*, dumping a portion of your allowance or your earnings into this one guilty pleasure. You read that comic in half an hour and threw it under the bed. As you grew, most of your childish toys and old magazines went out with the trash, but a few copies of *Little Lulu*—including the first edition—stayed with you. Your father never got a hold of it, and you kept it in mint condition.

When you turned 30, you read an article about comic book collectibles and were amazed to discover that some of them sell for thousands of dollars, so you dug out that old comic, took it to the store and discovered it was worth a fortune. Why? Because nobody else in the world had one. Supply and demand dictate the price, just like they do with everything else in the marketplace. You own something nobody else has, so the price is right.

Replace the comic book with an antique chair, a bottle of old wine, a Mickey Mantle rookie card or a Monet uncovered in your basement. The idea is the same: Many people make investments out of collectibles, but there is certainly no guarantee that anything will come of them.

These forms of investing have made people rich beyond their wildest dreams when all the variables went their way. No question about it: When you own a Mickey Mantle rookie card, you're probably not wanting for too much in this life. You've got collateral. If you happened to own the right piece of land at the right time, you'll probably swear by the value of real estate. I've never had much luck in that area.

You can make a fortune with any of these investments—and many more that I haven't bothered to mention. But for my money, for the walk-around, average, run-of-the-mill investor who is just looking to have a little more money tomorrow than he has today, the stock market is the place to be. And the statistics bear me out.

4

What's the Story?

Everyone who invests money in the stock market is looking for a chance to cash in on the next razor blade industry.

Razor blades? Are you kidding? But we're in the Information Age, you're saying to yourself. Technology is racing light years ahead of mankind's ability to use it, right? We have video cassette recorders, but no one knows how to set the clock on them. Computers are so advanced, only our children can use them without being intimidated. Our unmanned space probes are so complicated, even the rocket scientists can't control them. The telephone companies and newspapers are promising us movies, news and sports— whatever we want, whenever we want it at the touch of a button.

Surely, these are the areas where investors will find that pot of gold, right? Maybe, but I don't think so.

Smart investors want to find the next Gillette.

They want a product that you use a couple of times and throw away, something consumers will have to keep buying and buying and buying. They want a product that changes every few years just enough to keep consumers excited with each tiny advancement. And they want that product to come from a company that has virtually a corner on the market. So let's consider my example: Why does everyone want to find the next Gillette?

First of all, Gillette is king in the razor blade market. Nobody else comes close—certainly not Schick. Gillette rules 64 percent of the U.S. razor blade market. The rest divvy up what remains among themselves. So Gillette has one of our requirements covered pretty well. Nobody else can compete. In practical terms, there are really only two ways to shave. You can use a Gillette shaving system or you can use a sharp stone. Given a choice, most of us would prefer not to use a sharp stone. (Oh, there's electric shaving too, of course. And Gillette owns the Cadillac of electric razors: Braun.)

Let's back up a minute. I just used the phrase "Gillette shaving system" to describe what I'm talking about here. System? You thought we were just talking about a razor blade here, right? Think again. Before you lathered up your face (or your legs), you bought a razor blade *handle*, a package of replacement razor blades and a can of foam. Load up the handle with one of those blades, shave about a week, throw it away and load up another. A month later, you're back in the store for more blades. There's another one of our requirements for the perfect company. You need those blades for the rest of your life and once you start buying Gillette's, you're not likely to change.

But the fact is, you probably haven't been using the same shaving system for your whole life. Suppose you've been shaving for a long, long time. Maybe you started with Blue Blades, among the first decent replaceable razor blades ever invented. Finally, you didn't have to sharpen up a straight razor anymore. Slap on another Blue Blade and be done with it. Then you moved to Superblues in the 1960s. Then, in 1971, along comes the Trac II: a twin-blade cartridge that's easy to replace. Slide off the old blade cartridge and slide on the new one. Now Gillette is selling the Sensor, a flexible head designed to match the contours of your face. Perfect! Now we have all three requirements.

Maybe you loved the Trac II and the Sensor doesn't excite you. No problem; Gillette still makes it, and you can still buy it. But if each incremental change in shaving technology looks better than the last, then someone is going to buy it. And that's just in the United States. Gillette does 70 percent of its business outside North America.

A Close Shave for Gillette

In the mid-1980s, when takeover mania engulfed corporate America, Gillette was among the U.S. companies that found itself fighting off the raiders. The company fought off takeover artist Ronald Perelman three times, and it was successful each time, but not without paying a price. Gillette's last "victory" cost about $43 million. The company bought 9.2 million shares of its stock back from Perelman in November 1986 in exchange for his agreement to go away. It's known as "greenmail," the corporate world's version of blackmail.

Within a year, a new foe emerged. Coniston Partners, a triumvirate of takeover artists this time, made a run for control of Gillette's board of directors in late 1987 and early 1988. Most corporate takeovers work rather simply: Someone buys up enough stock to gain a majority share of the board of directors and the deed is done. Coniston wanted it another way: They simply wanted to persuade existing shareholders to give them the votes to take over the board of directors. Why? The promises were vague. They wanted to "maximize shareholder value." They didn't have definite plans—at least not any they were sharing. They wanted to make a lot of money for themselves.

At the time, we owned a little more than 2 percent of Gillette's stock. Two reasons: First, we always thought the Boston-based company was a good one; second, we heard the takeover speculation and thought there would be some money-making opportunities. Again, if Coniston had taken the usual takeover route, it would have paid shareholders a premium for their stock—and the privilege of owning the company. I've never objected to being paid more than I felt a stock was worth, and I would have sold my shares to Coniston if that was the way they had wanted to play it. But they didn't.

Coniston made its proposal at a shareholders meeting, asking shareholders to vote for their slate of directors on the board. Before the vote, executives from Coniston called every three or four days to lobby me with more vague promises and to ask how I would vote. *The Boston Globe* and *The Wall Street Journal* called too, but I wasn't telling. The vote was in April 1988; the results weren't known for almost two weeks.

Interestingly enough, no one from Gillette called. No one lobbied. Interesting, but not too surprising. Gillette had nothing to offer. If Gillette won, its stock price would almost certainly drop because the takeover speculation had inflated its value. If Gillette lost, its stock price would almost certainly rise. Coniston Partners would go in and sell off divisions of the company that weren't earning enough money. The proceeds from those sales could be used to buy back stock from shareholders. The stock price would rise.

In the end, I decided Coniston wasn't offering me anything. Besides that, I did not think every company in this country should have to worry about being taken over when they were doing a reasonable job, so we voted with the management of Gillette. The vote was 52 percent for Gillette, 48 percent for Coniston. Our 2 percent almost certainly made the difference.

I thought it was the right thing to do even though, as predicted, the stock price fell—almost $1.40 the day after the vote was announced. We lost some money at first, but the drop was not as bad as some had predicted. Eventually, it turned into a successful investment for us.

On this continent, we have the latest shaving system known to the world. Somewhere else on this earth, everything old is new again. Gillette is just now introducing the Trac II system to a society of shavers (that thinks it's great), and the company is getting another run for its money with what looks like old technology to us. Maybe somewhere, in an even more backwater part of the world, Blue Blades are all the rage. When Sensor becomes blasé here, it will be new somewhere else.

Now let's shift gears for a moment. There are three components to making money in the stock market. The first obviously is the market itself. Individual investors can't do much to affect the market as a whole. The second is the investor's choice of industries: retail, technology, utilities, drug companies, food companies or car companies? The last, of course, is the individual stock.

In some sense, Gillette is the Holy Grail of stock market companies. If you hitched your wagon to Gillette when we first bought it in November 1986 at $11.56 a share, you would have made almost 30 percent a year in the decade since. Gillette has shown years and years worth of staying power with a product that has a long, long, long shelf life—even when the product changes. If you buy stock in ABC Computer Co. just because it invents a new computer chip, you might make a few bucks, but not for long. XYZ Computer Co. will have another chip that's just as good or better in six months.

A long explanation for a simple concept, maybe. In a simple sense, this history is what investors are talking about when they ask, "What's the story?" They want to know about the company they may be investing in. Long-ball hitters in the Major Leagues know about the tale of the tape. High rollers in the stock market know they can't hit a home run unless they know the tale of the ticker tape. We've only discussed a somewhat abridged version of Gillette's story, but it begins to answer some of the questions investors have when they assemble "the story." What does the company do? Who manages the company? What's its track record? How have the company's earnings been in past years? How has the price of their stock changed? Has the company grown? How much, how fast? Who else does what this company does? Do they do it better or worse than the competitors?

INSIDE LINE

Among stock market investors, the phrase "what's the story" is repeated like a mantra whenever someone is trying to sell someone else on a particular stock. It is the fundamental question. The answer to that question determines whether you reach into your pocket, pull out some cash and buy stock in that company.

And like any story, there is a lot you need to know before you can decide whether you like it. We're talking about the details in this chapter, but here is a summary of some of the questions you'll need to answer:

Who are the characters? Who runs this company? Does the management team have a track record you can look at? Are the employees happy? Are there constant problems between labor and management? A good company is more likely to have happy employees.

What is the plot? What does the company do? What does it make? What are the company's earnings now and in the past? Has the company grown? How much? How fast? Who else does what this company does? Anyone do it better? I recommend that you stick with the companies that are among the top three in whatever they do.

What's the conflict? How much debt does the company carry? Remember, if you're carrying a mountain of debt, you're in bad shape if the car needs another set of tires or your air conditioner goes kaput. A company carrying too much debt is in the same boat. How has the company adjusted to changes in the economy? Has it shown a willingness to adapt and to adapt intelligently?

Read the book on any company that wants your money.

What's the story? If you can't answer that question, you don't know why you're buying a stock in the first place. You might as well be back at the race track. Investors who work that way are relying on what is known as the "Greater Fool Theory." They figure someone out there is a greater fool than they are. Someone will pay more for a stock than they did—for no reason at all. I've seen a lot of investors work that way.

As the old story goes, years ago a can of rare sardines was the chic investment oddity of the day. Today, it's old wine. Then, it was this can of sardines. The sardines changed hands every once in a while, each time trading at a higher and higher price. Finally, someone bought the sardines, opened the can and ate them. They were horrible. Of course they were bad, the investor was told; these sardines were for trading, not for eating.

That's a somewhat silly example of the "Greater Fool Theory." Here's a more realistic one:

In my first investment job, I worked in Fort Wayne, Indiana, at an insurance company that didn't have any stock quote machines when I started as a stock analyst for the company. During my lunch hour, I'd walk six blocks down to the local Merrill Lynch office to push a few buttons and find out how our stocks were doing. I'd see all manner of stock market investors stroll in and out at the same time. I'd see the farmers come in with their overalls on, talking with their brokers, buying and selling technology stocks. I would see the businessmen walk in wearing their suits and ties, buying and selling grain futures. I always found it particularly amusing. The farmers knew investing in grain futures was very speculative, and they didn't want to do it; the businessmen probably figured investing in technology was also a little too speculative. Those folks knew enough to know what *not* to buy. They just didn't know what they *should* buy. Throughout this book I will preach the same sermon: Buy what you know and know why you buy.

In fact, it wouldn't be a bad idea to write down the reasons why you bought stock in ABC Widgets on the day you bought it. We do it in my shop. I have books filled with page after page of analysts' reports that essentially detail why we bought a stock in the first place. We check the list from time to time. Are the reasons still valid? Does ABC still make widgets for the lowest cost per unit? Is the management still saintly? Have competitors crept into the widget market? If the reasons are still valid, you're probably fine. If not, you probably ought to take a second look.

I knew why I bought Kinder-Care in 1983. The company seemed to have everything going for it. Here we were in the mid-1980s, women were becoming a larger and larger share of the work force, and someone thought to establish a chain of day care centers around the country. It's a philosophy that works in retailing and fast food, why not child care? If you liked the Kinder-Care day care center in one part of the country, why wouldn't you like it somewhere else? Besides that, the company earnings were growing at 31 percent a year. In a word, I liked Kinder-Care's story.

How much? Here's what we wrote in our November 1983 report on the company: "Kinder-Care is the largest operator of private day care centers in the U.S. with an outstanding record and exceptional prospects for rapid growth. Kinder-Care has evolved over the past 15 years into the largest factor in the highly fragmented day care center business."

We gushed about the company's size, its revenue growth of 34 percent a year, its 800 day care centers in 37 states. We didn't have enough good things to say about the company. I liked it so much that I'd buy more stock when the price would dip from time to time. I ended up being the company's largest shareholder at one point.

Then in 1986, when the price of the stock started to founder a bit in the market, the management at Kinder-Care decided to strike out in an odd direction: They bought an insurance company. This should have been a tipoff, but for some reason, I wasn't paying attention. The question is obvious to you now, right? What possible business does a chain of child care centers have with an insurance company? I wish I'd asked the question at the time, but Kinder-Care's earnings continued to do okay, the stock continued to rise and fall, and when it dropped a lot, I still bought more.

Kinder-Care bought a Miami savings and loan company in 1987. More and more, Kinder-Care was becoming something that wasn't what I bought in the first place. Then more bad news started to trickle in. In 1989, the management began getting a bad reputation for making business decisions that benefitted them, not the company. The top executives became tangled up with the Drexel-Burnham Lambert junk bond mess in the late 1980s, buying hundreds of millions of dollars worth of junk bonds and driving Kinder-Care more deeply into debt. Finally, I woke up.

I arranged a meeting with the chief operating officer of the company. I met with him in Miami in 1989, and during that meeting, it became apparent that this company wasn't doing what I wanted it to do. I had lost confidence in the company, somewhat belatedly. Within days of that meeting, we sold every share of it from our funds. What did we have to say about Kinder-Care the last time we wrote about it?

"All of Kinder-Care's businesses are doing poorly. We cannot quantify how bad because management has little credibility. Our earnings-per-share estimate (of $.88), while it looks precise, is a wild guess. The stock has had two run-ups in the last month from $7.50 to $9. These are accompanied by rumors of a takeover which do not appear to have any validity. It's time to say good-bye to a very bad idea."

I was fortunate that I had the meeting at the time I did—and that I made the decision to sell. For some unknown reason, there was some positive activity, and Kinder-Care stock took a jump at the time I was selling out. I didn't lose as much as I might have, but I lost enough: I bought the stock at the equivalent of $12 a share after stock splits; I sold it at around $8.75 a share. Another reason I'm glad I got out when I did: A year later, the chief operating officer pleaded guilty to two counts of fraud. The company went bankrupt. (A note here about Kinder-Care: The day care centers have continued to flourish with new management and a new corporate structure. Remember: Child care was never a problem for Kinder-Care. All the mismanagement and unrelated enterprises were.)

With Kinder-Care, I violated one of my own cardinal rules of investing: Know why you're buying stock in a company, and know why you're continuing to hold it. When you do something right, you have to know why it was right; when you do something wrong, you have to know why it was wrong.

But what are you looking for? What makes a good story? Think of the last good movie you saw or the last good book you read. Were the characters in that story compelling? Was the plot engaging? A key part of any good drama is conflict. What was the conflict in your story? How was it resolved? A new investment possibility comes along, and you ask yourself that age-old question: "What's the story?" The answer could be compared to the drama you were just thinking about. Just take it apart and look at the individual pieces of the story.

Who are the characters in this company? Look at the management of the ABC Widget Co. Have they done good things before with other companies? What are they doing with the company you're looking at? Find a copy of the company's prospectus or its last report to shareholders and look at the company's balance sheet. How much debt has your cast of characters run up with the ABC Widget Co.? Divide the company's long-term debt by its assets to figure the debt ratio. A company with a very high debt ratio may be in trouble. I'd avoid any company that has more than 50 percent debt. The higher the debt ratio, the less flexibility your company has in bad times. You can't buy a house if you're maxed out on your credit cards and paying off a couple of cars, right? A debt-ridden company can't afford to expand with new stores or develop new products if it's paying off debt instead. You might also look at another piece of the cast: management's relationship with labor. Any company that has good labor relations has another check mark in the plus column. Are the employees made to feel that they are a part of the company? Do they share in the successes of the company—the financial successes? If the managers are doing a good job, they are trying to maximize the wealth of the company's shareholders. If the company's employees are among the shareholders, they have a stake in the company's successes.

How about the plot? What does your company do? We've been talking about a widget company. Is it a good product? I recommend that you stick with the companies that are among the top three in their industry, those that have shown a strong track record. Are the company's costs low? It will be more important in the '90s than it was in the '80s, when the economy was booming and a company practically had to work *not* to grow. These days, after the go-go '80s, low costs will streamline your company and help it grow. Example: General Electric. A classic example of a company with an average product line, yet it continues to grow 10-plus percent a year because its operation is extremely efficient—and it gets more efficient every year.

How about the drama? the conflict? How has your company adjusted to change in the economy? in its market? A company that has shown a willingness and an ability to change is usually a good bet. Gillette is a good example: The company has constantly come out with new products, and it has improved what it already has. Not just Blue Blades anymore, right? It's the same story with Procter & Gamble. Not many companies can boast a product like Tide, which has been the number one laundry detergent since we stopped beating our clothes against rocks to get them clean. But that hasn't stopped P&G from offering improved versions of Tide or bubble-gum flavored Crest for children.

These are the kinds of questions you need to ask—and answer—as you assemble the story of your latest investment possibility. It's a good idea to do your homework on a stock ahead of time, so if there is an opportunity, you're ready. If you've been following Wal-Mart, or the retail industry in general, and there is news about it, you are ready. That doesn't mean you don't do more work, but if you're ready, you're better off.

I'm fortunate to have done a lot of homework over the years, so I'm ready when a blockbuster investment opportunity comes along. They don't very often. Few stories impress me so much the first time I hear them that I run out and buy the stock immediately. Blockbuster Entertainment impressed me. Here was a company capitalizing on a major trend in the United States. Marketing mavens call it "cocooning." You and I just call it "spending the evening at home." Now we had another good reason to stay at home: Every movie ever made was coming out on videotape before the movie-house popcorn could get stale. And there was Blockbuster, gobbling up every mom-and-pop videotape store in the country. I don't think I had ever rented a video at the time, but I was listening.

Blockbuster had several things in its corner. Its president, H. Wayne Huizenga, had started in business with a few garbage trucks. He wheeled and dealed until he merged with another garbage hauler and helped turn it into a multimillion dollar company called Waste Management—maybe you've heard of it. It's only the largest waste hauler in the country.

For me, the clincher had less to do with Huizenga than with the folks he hired for Blockbuster. One of the major players in the company had been in charge of picking sites for new McDonald's restaurants. At my breakfast meeting one morning, an investment analyst told me that this guy knew every intersection in the country. With fast food, and I assumed with fast fun, location is everything. I finished my breakfast. I went to my office. By 10 A.M., I was a shareholder.

BYE-BYE BLOCKBUSTER

In a tearful farewell to shareholders in September 1994, Wayne Huizenga thanked shareholders for their vote to merge his baby, Blockbuster Entertainment, into Viacom, the mammoth book, movie, video production and film company. The resulting company—which also included an earlier merger with Paramount—created the second largest entertainment company on earth, second only to Time Warner.

A majority of Blockbuster shareholders had voted for the merger, giving up their Blockbuster stock in exchange for several varieties of Viacom's stock. I was not among the majority.

When a company is a takeover target, shareholders typically expect to get a premium for their stock. If it's so good that someone wants to buy it all, stockholders reason, we ought to make some good money on it. I don't think that happened with Blockbuster. Shareholders weren't getting cash for their Blockbuster stock, they were getting Viacom stock, the value of which dropped while the negotiations labored along. I thought Blockbuster stock was worth at least $35 a share at the time, but by the time it finally happened, the package was worth $26 a share. Three months later, the value of my Viacom holdings was only $28.

A similar story involves Cott Corp., a sleepy little company that nobody ever paid any attention to. Then, Cott bought the rights to bottle Royal Crown Cola under private labels. Great! They're going to bottle a brand of cola that has never been able to compete with the big boys, Coca-Cola and Pepsi. So what's the big deal?

In a word, they found a niche. The company started bottling RC Cola for other stores like Safeway and Wal-Mart. Then they slapped a store's brand name on the label, something like Sam's Cola. And instead of selling low-cost, lousy-tasting soft drinks, Wal-Mart and other stores like it can sell a low-cost, good-tasting cola. Sam's promotes it aggressively, sells it at steep discounts, and their market share is growing fantastically. In Canada, they have a 27 percent market share in the grocery stores. Their sales in Canada were doubling every year.

We first bought it in July 1992 at $5.50 a share. A year later, it's price hit $37. And like any good story, the second chapter is better than the first: Cott signed deals to expand into the Europe. Unfortunately, subsequent chapters weren't so great. Sales were still good, but Cott struggled to keep earnings up. By chapter four, we had sold 60 percent of our holdings as Cott dropped to $10 a share. Chapter five is yet to be written: The company is trying to do with beer, tea, water, and other consumer products what it did with cola. I hope so!

You can see that being plugged in ahead of time gives you a big jump. I should have taken my own advice the first time I went to The Home Depot. My wife climbed up on our old ladder and the steps broke. I had a choice: Get a new wife or get a new ladder. So I found The Home Depot.

From the first time you go to The Home Depot, you know it's a great concept. You've been to hardware stores before. You've been to lumber yards. You've been to home-and-garden shops. But The Home Depot is different, it's exciting. It's all of them under one roof. The customers look happy when they're shopping there (but I know as soon as they get home, they have to work all day on that leaky faucet or balky sprinkler system). You walk up and down every aisle just to see what kinds of tools and gadgets you can buy for your house. The ladder is the last thing you look for. And next week, you want to do the same thing again. The only thing that could mess up this concept is bad management. The Home Depot doesn't have it. Instead, The Home Depot grew at least 30 percent a year for a decade, it has superior management and the best investory and supply system in the industry. So why did we miss the ride?

At first, we didn't. We owned the stock for a while as it climbed higher and higher until we decided it had become overpriced. We thought it had peaked, and we sold the stock. Wrong. It hadn't peaked. It kept going up, and it left us behind. We waited years for a chance to buy it again. By mid-1993, the stock was selling for around $50 a share. Then in September 1993, it slipped. It fell into the $40 range; a major investment house downgraded its growth estimate for the company. That hurt the stock some more, dropping it five points in one day that month. That's when we said, "This is the buying opportunity." Nothing was wrong with The Home Depot. Its management hasn't changed and the recession was over (as if the recession had hurt the company?). We started buying it at $37 a share. The price fell another point and a half and we pulled out our bushel baskets, scooping up as much of The Home Depot's stock as we could find.

Why? Simple. We had done our homework on The Home Depot—eight years' worth. We knew a good story when we heard it. That's fine, but it's meaningless if you don't *act on it*. At the time, we expected The Home Depot to grow 30 percent a year.

Doing the homework now means you catch the stars just before they are rising—or you can jump off before they fall. It may sound obvious, but the more homework you've done ahead of time, the more likely you are to profit. If you wait until everyone else has jumped aboard a good idea, you're too late. You must own a stock before every analyst on the planet recommends it. Otherwise, everyone will start buying it, the price will go up and you will have missed part of the ride.

A good way to fail in the stock market is to be timid. Successful investors make decisions. They believe in their ability. If you think something is a good idea, it probably is. Just be sure you read the story.

And be sure to be realistic about your prospects. Everyone wants the Holy Grail of stocks. They want to be the first shareholder of a company that is destined for long-term growth and profit. But as usual, the bottom line is the bottom line. Even the best story isn't worth reading if the price is too high. The key is knowing the right price when you see it.

5

A Day in the Life

I generally consider myself to be a man of considerable discipline. I pay cash for my cars. I spend as little as possible on clothes without dressing like a slob. I exercise. But about 10 years ago, I allowed myself to be caught up in what could only be described as The Great Cookie War. It served as a reminder of how I do business differently from some of the other fund managers in my profession—and why I'm perfectly happy to continue doing business my way.

The Great Cookie War was a war to win over the sweet tooth of America, a war waged in the kitchens of Big Food. Among the key combatants, of course, were Nabisco and Keebler, Procter & Gamble (with its Duncan Hines division) and Pepsico, each fighting the other to be the rightful heir to your grandmother's cookie recipe. And the latest ammunition in this war was something unseen on the shelves of your local supermarket before: the soft cookie—chewy, pliable, soft. The first battlefield in this war was Kansas City, where it seemed all the cookie companies were test marketing their new soft cookies. Relenting to my weakness, I sampled the fare from every front of this cookie war and determined that Keebler had the best soft cookie. Theirs was the cookie that would turn the heads of supermarket shoppers, translating into big profits for the company and a detriment to Nabisco.

I sold all my stock in Nabisco.

Big mistake. Not only did Nabisco win the cookie war, but the company was later bought out in one of the largest corporate take-overs in history. Nabisco stocks soared. Then I realized what I should have known at the very beginning: Keebler's cookies are usually better than Nabisco's; they just don't sell as well—never have. I let myself do original research on a company, and it clouded my judgment.

That's not usually my style. I don't usually have time for original research when I'm deciding how to invest money. I usually don't sample new foods, call corporate executives or sleep in new motel chains just to get a sampling of the company. I'm not interested in doing a lot of jet-setting around the country. I rarely make visits to corporate headquarters. That doesn't mean original research is bad— it's just not me.

And that's what analysts are for. My day usually starts with the people who earn a lot of money to do the research for me. I talk to a dozen representatives from some of the best-known brokerage houses in the country: Goldman Sachs, Paine Webber, Smith Barney, Merrill Lynch. These people represent the views of their analysts who track companies in almost every industry—health care, energy, packaged foods, clothing, airlines, autos, you name it. Usually, I meet an analyst for breakfast at about seven in the morning. But before you get the wrong idea, just remember: On average, the research you get from Wall Street analysts is just that—average. Come to think of it, the breakfasts are about average as well.

So I start this morning with an analyst who covers drug companies, and right away he and I both know he has credibility problems. He's been clinging to the industry, recommending companies all the way while their stocks continue to sink. Any analyst has credibility as long as he or she is right. This one was wrong.

The parade of investment advice continues when I get to my office by 8:30 on the eighth floor of the SunBank tower in Orlando. A wall of windows looks out over Orange Avenue into a canyon of other bank buildings. I am around the corner from the city's budding Church Street Station entertainment district and about 20 minutes from Disney World, but there is enough entertainment on my desk to keep me busy for the next 10 hours. My window onto Wall Street, 1,500 miles away, is a speaker phone and an oversized computer quotation screen. As far as I'm concerned, my view of the investment capital of the world is as good as anyone else's. It has all the access of a seat on the New York Stock Exchange without the shoving on the floor or the winter cold on the street. From my vantage point, I can see every stock I care about, represented on that computer screen. The screen winks at me endlessly throughout the day every time a stock is traded, blue if the price went up, pink if it went down. But none of that has begun yet. Before the stock market opens for the day, I'm fielding more calls from brokerage houses in New York City, stabbing one button, then another as representatives check in before the opening bell.

The morning really doesn't get moving until the market opens, and the traders start making their calls. Today, I am eager to see what happens to Allstate Insurance, a subsidiary of Sears that has just become a publicly owned company. Sears sold $2 billion worth of stock, the largest public offering in history. As a large institutional trader, I have an opportunity to put in for an allocation when such massive offerings come across. This time around, I did well: one million shares in my portfolio, starting at $27 a share. Early in the day, a trader calls offering to buy as much as I'll sell for $28 a share. Make a quick million? No thanks. I'd like to see what happens to the stock before I jump into something. At the moment, I plan to be in this one for the long term—or $35 a share, whichever comes first. I think that's about as high as the stock is going to go, at least in the short term.

He calls later about an unrelated trade.

"How much of that Allstate did I sell you?" I ask.

"You didn't sell me any." He sounds slightly confused.

"Oh, is that right? I guess you didn't have your bag open."

He concedes he was trying to pull a fast one and says he's offering $1.75 more a share than the opening price. That puts him up to $28.75 a share.

"For you, 32," I tell him. The conversation is over. He gets the point: If you're looking to make a slick deal, make sure I'm not on the other side of the table.

That was a long conversation. Most of my telephone conversations last less than 20 seconds. The market isn't opened long enough in a day to spend time chitchatting with traders. Most of them understand that.

"We downgraded Synoptics. I don't think you care."

"Nope." One call down.

"Tony, I've got 50 Waste Management for sale if you care." That's 50,000 shares of the stock.

"No, thanks." Two calls down.

That's more like it. Get to the point. Make it quick. Let me go. There's always another deal to be made, and when the opportunity arises to do something big, you have to be ready for it.

"Tony, this is Paddins. I have a large seller of Air Products. I just want to know if you're interested right now. I can get back to you with some details."

Sure, I'm interested.

That call comes early in the day, within an hour of the opening bell. Someone somewhere is interested in selling nearly 1 million shares of Air Products, an industrial gas and chemical company that has been doing okay by my reckoning. The company's earnings are on the rise, and its shares have sold as high as $49 several times during the year. Right now, I punch a few buttons on my computer and discover it is trading at about $44 a share. But that's not the good news. The next time Paddins calls, he's asking $41.50 a share for the block of stock. The seller wants to unload a large chunk of this stock at a $2.5 million discount to the market price. And I can't find anything wrong with the merchandise. Suppose you had $100 burning a hole in your pocket. If a salesman raced up the aisle and begged you to pay half price for a flawless $100 cashmere sweater, what would you do? Of course! Offer less than the asking price.

I bid $41.25 a share—$.25 cheaper—for 500,000 shares and agreed to pay his asking price of $41.50 for the rest. Paddins signs off to make another call. I'm standing behind my desk now. I don't think I've ever made such a large trade before. The phone rings shortly past noon. It's Paddins calling again. This time the ploy didn't work. The seller is sticking with his wildly deflated asking price. The deal is done. In the end, I purchased 845,000 shares in a good company in a decent industry. Only time will tell if I am right, of course. Right now, I'm feeling moderately brilliant. If the stock jumped a point in the next few days, I'd feel really brilliant. Everyone in the office will be talking about today's near million-share purchase. But now, it's time for lunch. A salad in the company cafeteria.

Ninety-eight cents. Always the frugal gourmet.

Of course, million-share trades don't happen every day. More than likely, the day is spent charting a course through the daily eddies and currents of the stock market. For example, we have spent months navigating our shares in Fruit of the Loom through lower Manhattan's river of money. We first began buying the stock in 1990 when it was selling for nearly $12 a share. Almost immediately, the stock dropped in half. But remember the advice I have already given so many times: Don't bail out if you think you're right. Hold your ground. Consider your position: Is there anything materially wrong with the company? It is a theme I will repeat again and again. In this case, the answer was no. Nothing had changed to sour me on Fruit. The only difference? The chief executive officer and major shareholder had major financial problems—not the company, but its captain. Time proved me right: The stock went back up to $21 a share shortly after that and more than doubled a year later. It peaked at $50 two and a half years after that.

But on this day, Fruit of the Loom has found itself in rough seas again, providing another opportunity to test my skills at the helm—at least where my holdings are concerned. Remember: It's every investor for himself. The stock is down to $30 a share, and my colleagues are wondering why we don't abandon ship. Meanwhile, one of my staff analysts dashes into my office with word that Fruit has offered another 1.5 million shares of stock. Is the company foundering that badly? Does it need extra cash to keep itself afloat? My staff tells me to consider jumping ship; Sara Lee, the company that owns Hanes, would love to take us aboard, they say. I don't argue; Hanes is a good company too. But I don't think it is time to give up on Fruit of the Loom yet. Again, why give up on a company that is undervalued if there is nothing materially wrong with it? That might be the time to buy more!

In this case, on this day, there is something materially wrong with Fruit of the Loom: The company just has too much of it. Material, that is. The company has more T-shirts than it knows what to do with. When sales rose a year earlier, the company found itself without enough production capacity to meet the demand. The company expanded its capacity, but the market didn't expand fast enough to absorb all the extra cotton underwear. Definitely a problem, but not one I'm ready to lose sleep over. The phone rings; another trader asks about Fruit of the Loom. We both know about the excess T-shirts. He tells me about the 1.5 million shares of new stock that were just offered.

"You're kidding," I say, feigning surprise. I'm really looking for new information. "Is it new stock?"

"It's just a headline at the moment," he replies. "I've got a buyer."

"Okay."

Of course he has a buyer. Why else would he be calling? But I'm not interested in selling. I'm not so alarmed by Fruit's bloated T-shirt inventory that I'm going to jump into a bad deal. And as for the additional 1.5 million shares of stock? Well, that story wasn't as bad as it sounded. The company wasn't offering *new* shares of the stock. Remember our bankrupt CEO from two years earlier? He simply sold some of *his* stock back to the company; the only way he could get a loan, I suppose. I'll keep my shares of Fruit of the Loom for now, thank you very much.

And four months later, when sales continue to slow down and Fruit of the Loom still can't get rid of its inventory, I sell them. You can't always be right.

That episode is an example of how an investor's focus can be different, but the philosophy doesn't change. Your view of the stock market will be a lot different from mine. I'm watching the day-to-day changes in a company or an industry. Sometimes, I'm even watching the changes minute by minute, and I can capitalize on the tiny interim changes that affect the price of one stock or another. Unless all you do is watch the stock market, you probably won't notice the blips the way I do—and there is no reason you should. In the stock market, every day has its ups and downs. So does every week, every quarter, every year. Your focus on the market will be different from mine. In the end, the philosophy is the same. Consider the Fruit of the Loom example: I could notice and react to a daily blip on the company's radar screen because my focus is very tight. At the same time, I look at the bigger picture. I had been watching Fruit of the Loom for more than two years by the time this little blip came along.

I have been watching food companies for a long time too. For many years, I was known in the industry as the king of food company investors. You buy their mayonnaise, their taco sauce, their crackers. I bought their stocks and did just fine swapping among CPC International, the makers of Hellmann's Real Mayonnaise; and Nabisco, the makers of those so-so soft cookies; and Kellogg; and Ralston. So I'm not altogether unhappy to break my own rule when executives from Nabisco schedule a meeting next week. A decade ago, Nabisco was a commodity in one of the early corporate takeovers of the 1980s; on this day, its owners (the Reynolds tobacco people) want to put Nabisco back in the stock market. They want to sell Nabisco stock again. Am I interested, they want to know? I'll be happy to tell them when they come. But I make them promise to bring some chocolate-covered Oreos—ah, that blasted weakness! They are wonderful cookies, I will tell them, but they are overpriced. The Nabisco executives do me one better. A package arrives one week before the meeting, stuffed with Nabisco products: Grey Poupon mustard, Stelladora cookies, Fig Newtons, Planter's peanuts (with hot spice!), Bubble Yum gum, Mr. Phipps Pretzel Chips and—of course—Oreo cookies. Not the chocolate-covered kind.

And in the end, Nabisco never did offer that stock. Too bad. At the price that I bid them for 3 million shares, it would have been a great investment.

6

Us and Them

In Omaha, Nebraska, I lived hundreds of miles away from the nearest Major League baseball team—a definite disadvantage when you're a kid. Omaha had a minor league team at the time, a single-A farm club for the St. Louis Cardinals—enough of a connection that I became a big Stan Musial fan. But I was looking for my own Major League team to root for.

Pure serendipity decided which teams my brother and I would claim as our own. During an excursion to Woolworth's, my brother and I ran across souvenir billfolds on one of the racks, each bearing the likeness of a pro baseball player. I was nine years old. It was 1948. My brother found the rack first, so he laid claim to the last remaining Joe DiMaggio billfold. He became the Yankees fan. I dug through the pile and found a Ted Williams billfold—a player I had never heard of at the time, believe it or not. I've been a Boston Red Sox fan ever since—in spite of the 1949 pennant race. And the 1950 pennant race. And the 1951 pennant race. . . .

As a kid, I was a baseball nut. I could have named the starting lineup for every Major League team. I remembered stats and standings. Although I haven't followed baseball since Ted Williams retired more than 30 years ago, I did maintain a long-distance relationship with the Red Sox for many years back then—but I've never lived in Boston. As a kid, I could follow the games and the players on a transistor radio and I could read box scores in the newspapers. Later, I had television. And as any Red Sox fan will tell you, there is no shortage of people to commiserate with, anywhere in the United States. It wasn't that hard to root for a ball team that was 2,000 miles away.

In a sense, I have done the same thing with my job for the past three decades. In my line of work, the biggest playing field is located in lower Manhattan. The stats and standings are published in the newspaper every day, and I can watch the game from a computer screen in my office. The analogy falls down a bit thanks to one major difference: I can play the game from my office too. And I can play it as well as (or better than) anyone in the stadium. The point, of course, is that you can too.

There are a few things you and I have in common as stock market investors. For one thing, the chances are pretty good you don't live in New York City either. You probably live hundreds of miles from the so-called hub of world commerce. You probably have a life outside the office, unlike so many of the corporate MBA-types who haunt the investment houses and brokerages that line Wall Street, devoting a dozen hours or more a day in the pursuit of the Almighty Dollar. You probably don't have access to corporate CEOs who will answer the phone when you call and explain why their company's stock just fell five points. I might be able to do that, but the fact is, I don't want to.

New York City in general, and the stock market in particular, is jammed with thousands of analysts, traders, brokers and accountants with MBA degrees who think those extra two years of college give them a head start on investments. Many of them think they're better off. Some even think we're ignorant hayseeds so baffled by their world that we couldn't make money with a crystal ball. I recall an aerospace analyst in New York who worked for a major brokerage. He wouldn't come to see me or my staff to discuss any investment opportunities because he thought all southerners lived in the back woods somewhere. A lot of good his MBA did him; he alienated an entire office full of investors with billions of dollars to spend.

I've got a master's degree too—in mathematics. I could argue my job has as much to do with understanding numbers as it does with understanding business. I could, but I won't. The fact is, understanding investments has more to do with making investments than studying about making investments. I took an investment class in college once. I got a *C*. The high point of the class was the one and only paper I wrote. The term paper had to describe what makes the stock market move. I pored over stock market tables in the University of Iowa library before I started to write. My thesis went something like this: If you see the market rise 10 percent (or whatever number I found at the time), that confirms an upward trend. That's the time to buy into the market. When the market declines as a whole 10 percent (or whatever), that's the time to sell and stay out until it rises 10 percent again from the new low.

I tracked this trend over a 30-year period. It was phenomenally successful. My professor thought it was so interesting, he accused me of plagerizing it. It would have predicted the Crash of 1929. You could have made money in the 1929–33 period.

And, of course, it was complete hooey. I made it up based on some numbers I'd found in the stock market tables. It also defies my current philosophy: Stay invested all the time.

So it is somewhat difficult to take the MBAs too seriously.

Besides, who needs the lifestyle? Does it take you two hours to get to work every day? Do you take hours of work home with you, sweating away without a vacation? Me neither.

It takes me 12 minutes to get to work in the morning. I'm usually at work by 7:00 or 7:30 in the morning. For the New York crowd to show up that early, they'd have to wake up in the middle of the night every day to make the train. Too many people take this line of work too seriously. They spend 12 hours in the office and carry home armloads of reports to read. I could do that too. But I don't. When I leave the office—usually by 5 P.M.—I leave most of my work there. I have read about and heard about high-finance business people who are classic workaholics, toiling away every day of every week without a vacation. I take vacations. Even better, I don't bother calling the office when I'm away. I don't call and I don't worry. That's why they call it a vacation. What could I do anyway?

They need to wine and dine investors, jetting around the country to make appointments to "do" lunch. Their firms lay out huge sums of money for food and golf outings and trips designed to coax investors to buy certain stocks or do business with certain brokerage houses. When Euro Disney opened in France a few years ago, I actually had brokers inviting me to attend the grand event. I live in Orlando. Why on earth would I need to attend the opening of another Disney theme park? I don't need to go on their trips or eat their food any more than you do. Most of the time, I turn them down.

A refreshing trend is starting to show up in the securities business. Folks who work in the industry are beginning to discover what you and I already know: The investment world does not begin and end on Wall Street. In 1970, about half of all the people who worked in the securities industry worked in New York City. Twelve years later, that number was down to 30 percent. The experts are calling it an exodus. Money managers and brokerage firms are finding they can be just as successful in the Rocky Mountains of Colorado as they can in the glass canyons of Manhattan.

That doesn't mean there aren't advantages to working in New York. Obviously, it is still the nerve center for the stock market and hundreds of analysts swarm around Wall Street like angry bees. If I were there, analysts would probably stop by all the time to chat, fill me in on the latest. It might be nice to have access to the information face-to-face. That doesn't mean the information is necessarily moving any faster. The point is not that I have a professional *advantage* living in Orlando. The point is that it's not a *disadvantage* to be here instead of there. I get all the service I want. It's easy for people to come and see me.

And, of course, technology is a great equalizer.

As long as you have a telephone (and telephone lines), you have access to as much information as you need. Information goes anywhere; it is instantaneous. Newspapers and computer bulletin boards offer almost up-to-the-minute stock quotes on any publicly traded company. How much information you want or need is entirely up to you.

In three decades of investing, I've only been to the New York Stock Exchange once, in 1985. Frankly, nothing impressed me about it. It was interesting, but I doubt I'd go again. It left me wondering how anything gets done at all. Traders are scrambling around the floor of the exchange carrying tickets, waving their paper wares at specialists at the trading posts. The whole thing looks frantic and bustling, but I didn't get the sense I was at the center of world capitalism.

I'd rather visit the Smithsonian Institution in Washington, D.C. than make another trip to the New York Stock Exchange.

7

Sizing Things Up

I wouldn't blame you for being just a little skeptical about anything you've read so far. You've got a full-time job, earning money to support your family and your lifestyle. Your personal investment goals are a lot different from my professional ones. I'm working with 4 billion bucks. You might be working with several thousand. I'm spending every minute of the business day charting stocks, monitoring companies. You're going to spend Sunday afternoon mulling your investment opportunities over coffee and the morning newspaper. Why would anything I say be relevent to you?

That's what we'll discuss here. We've already spent some time discussing some of the things we have in common. But let's face it: There are a lot of things we don't have in common. I do this full time, for example. I probably have a lot more time than you do to spend watching the stock market. Does investment advice from a professional money manager translate into something an individual investor can use? I've got some advantages—pretty bigs ones actually—that you probably don't have. You wouldn't believe me if I denied it. But you've got a lot of advantages simply because you

63

will likely be working with less money than I am. If you're not, you probably don't need my advice anyway.

The fact is, you're probably a lot better off than I am in several ways. My investment strategy is sound. It works for me—but it worked a lot better when my portfolio was smaller. It's a jungle out there, right? Well, investors like me lumber through the jungle slowly, plodding our way from tree to tree. We're the woolly mammoths, stomping through a jungle of investment opportunities. We can't sneak up on one of those trees because our footfalls give us away. We can't be satisfied feeding off one tree—we need a whole thicket full of them. When I succeed in grabbing one investment opportunity, another giant jungle dweller has to fail.

Individual investors don't have those concerns. They're the small animals scurrying around under the tree canopy, scooting from tree to tree in that jungle, grabbing a few leaves here and there before they dart to another one. There's plenty for everyone there. The individual investors can do just fine, oblivious to what the mammoths are up to (see Figure 7-1).

The Institutional Investor Vs. the Individual

My Disadvantages	Your Advantages
I'm working with a lot of money; I can't move fast, can't always find a buyer or a seller.	You're working with less money; that makes you more nimble as an investor. You can move quickly in and out of opportunities.
I tend to spread the money around throughout an industry; can't just pick a single performing stock.	You can afford to invest in only the best companies; I must spread the wealth.
I must report to investors and the SEC. Everyone knows how I did yesterday.	There's always a buyer for your stock.
Day-to-day trends are vital; I must watch like a hawk.	You have no one to answer to but yourself.

Fig. 7-1

Frankly, the stock market penalizes the mammoths. The penalty is so great, in fact, that some money managers can't even be bothered trying to compete with other investors. Some pension funds, for example, hook their fortunes to the stock market as a whole. It's called indexing. Those fund managers might buy stock in companies that mirror the makeup of the Standard & Poor's 500 stock index, for example. If that index does well, so does the pension fund; if not, well, those are the breaks. A fund that big can never do worse than the stock market as a whole. Of course, it can't do better either. You and I can.

But it's getting tougher for me. I'll give you an example, but let's turn back to that Sunday morning newspaper for a second.

Remember when I mentioned that *everything* has some connection to the stock market? Well, grab that pile of coupon inserts and advertisements, the ones that you usually throw away when you rifle through the Sunday paper. Along the edge of some of them, you'll probably see the name Valassis. That's the company that prints those coupons and sends them out to newspapers all over the country. For a long time, they were virtually the only ones doing it.

In mid-1992, we had a small position in the company—small for us, that is. A million shares of stock isn't small, but it made up a tiny percentage of our holdings at the time.

So there we were, with our million shares valued at about $23 million, when suddenly a competitor entered the market. No problem, we said. This new company is poorly financed. It will go away, we thought. It didn't. Somewhere, they came up with a big infusion of cash, enough to jump-start their operations and wreck Valassis's stock. In the space of a few weeks, Valassis's stock lost more than half its value, falling from $23 a share to $11 a share. And there we were with one million of them.

Where do you sell a million shares of stock, especially when it's rarely traded in the first place, and all the news about it is bad? If we had brought that many shares to the market at one time, the price would have fallen even more. It would have destroyed the stock. I don't like to plunge a dagger into a stock that I own; I won't pay up for a stock when I buy it, and I won't sell down a stock I want to get rid of. I ended up eating the loss for a while, until I could sell my shares in dribs and drabs, squeezing as much value as I could out of every share. It wouldn't have been that way 10 years ago. I probably wouldn't have owned a million shares, and I probably could have sold 100,000 of them fairly easily.

Double lesson there: First, I can't sell my position in a stock fast; second, I can't really afford to be investing in a single company all the time. What do I mean by that?

You can invest your money in 10 or 20 individual stocks when you're pulling together your portfolio. For the individual investor, that's a respectable portfolio—diverse enough to protect the investments, yet small enough to manage them. If you like banks, for example, and you think they will prosper, you can buy stock in the one or two you expect will prosper the most. I can't. If I like banks, I have to like the whole banking industry. I need to buy stock in 12 of them and hope they do better than the 80 I don't own. I need to hope banking as a whole does well. On the other hand, if I think banking is a lousy industry right now, and I'm right, I avoid the whole thing. Let everyone else take a bath in banking, I'd say. I'll stay high and dry.

None of this is to say that I'm some pathetic creature, barely eking out a living in the stock market. You have your advantages, I have mine. Let's consider some of mine, some of yours and how you can overcome the ones you don't have.

When was the last time someone called you with news about a company you thought might be a good investment? Or with the inside scoop, the statistics and numbers that you hadn't read in the newspaper or your financial magazine yet? That's probably my biggest advantage: I've got lots of advice. My computer is plugged into the Big Board in New York, so I know what is happening to any stock at any time with the touch of a button. I can get the news of the day instantly on my computer, before it comes out in the morning newspaper or the evening news. My phone rings constantly with folks who want to feed me the latest line from their stable of stock analysts. We deal with 14 stock brokerage firms; I have access to as many as 700 analysts who spend their time learning every little thing about all the major companies on earth. How has Kmart changed its advertising campaign? Is that likely to boost its market share against Wal-Mart? Why is Waste Management reporting a loss this quarter? What will Fruit of the Loom do with all its extra T-shirts and will that affect the earnings for Sara Lee, which owns Hanes?

The fact is, nobody calls you on the phone and says, "This is what we know and this is what it means." How does it help me?

You might have read in the newspapers a few years back that General Motors was losing market share to the other domestic auto makers. Alarming, wasn't it? On top of all the other troubles GM was having—an executive coup at the top, tremendous losses, plant closings, poor labor relations—the darn company couldn't even sell its share of cars anymore. We read the same things in the newspaper.

This was alarming to us because we had started buying GM stock in late 1991. The country was coming out of the recession, and we figured folks were about ready to start buying those new cars finally. Auto stocks are cyclical, meaning their fortunes tend to rise and fall with the economy. Beyond that, they are typically early cycle stocks: When the economy starts to nose-dive, they're usually among the first to feel it; when the economy improves, they are among the first to benefit. But why buy GM? After all, they were having all that bad news. True, they were the poorest managed company, but management was improving. Basically, they had nowhere to go but up. In 1992, the CEO of GM had been ousted; management brought in a head that had a very strong background in cutting costs, and they started to make substantial cost savings and cost cuttings. At the same time, the auto industry as a whole was finally turning around, some of GM's models started selling well, and the foreign car industry was having troubles.

And the loss of market share? No big problem. Instead of selling a whole lot of autos—at very low prices—to places like rental car companies, GM focused on selling to you. Fleet sales aren't particularly profitable. GM makes a lot more money per car on you than it does on a rental car company. And among individual buyers, GM's market share was rising.

In 1993, GM's stock price went from $32 to $60.

All this information came to us through Wall Street contacts who were in touch with General Motors on a weekly basis: plant closings, profit per car, market share among foreign auto makers—all of it. A lot of this was available to you too. But there's no getting around the fact that I'm going to know a lot more of the pertinent information—me and all the other woolly mammoths wandering around the jungle. That certainly doesn't mean you ought to run away and hide.

You'll use your advantages. One of them, for example, would be the fact that you don't need to worry what happens to GM—or any other stock, for that matter—from one day to the next. I spend 50 hours a week watching the stock market and all the stocks I've bought. It's my business to know the meaning of every quarter-point shift in a stock's price. I've got a very good reason for that. In fact, it's one of my disadvantages.

If I make a mistake, which I probably do 48 percent of the time, everybody sees it. Open up the business section of the paper and you can find out how Tony Gray did yesterday. Lots of people are watching my performance. You don't have to go to cocktail parties and justify all your losing stock ideas; I do. Your job probably doesn't depend on how your portfolio did last quarter. Your fortunes might, but not your job. Mine does. There is usually a lot of pressure on me to get rid of my mistakes—the bad stocks in my portfolio—so I don't compound the error.

I learned that lesson early in my career, when I managed individual investor accounts at a suburban Chicago bank. Every three months, I met with one of my clients, a woman who would pore over the list of stocks I had bought and sold since the last time we talked. Without fail, she would settle on the stock that had done the worst and gripe endlessly about why it was still there. I tried to explain to her that it didn't make any difference what was in her portfolio—*something* would always be the worst performer in the bunch. She was not a very agreeable client, so she wasn't particularly receptive to this argument.

That leads to another reason why I'm so conscious of the day-to-day fluctuations in Wall Street. As an individual investor, you can and should be less interested in those short-term fluctuations in the stock market. You can take more of a long-term position. I am constantly dogged by the numbers in the papers, however, and I need to capitalize on changes in the market as soon as I can.

There is yet another reason why my slavish attention to the stock market is an advantage to me, but not a disadvantage for you. Individual investors, by and large, are trading against the Big Board. There's always a buyer for their stock. Nobody knows if they buy or sell shares in ABC Widgets. But in my business, I'm competing with a lot of other woolly mammoths out there. I'm trading tens and hundreds of thousands of shares in a company. If I want to sell some stock, I need to find someone who wants to buy it. And suppose I buy a stock and the price goes up a few bucks right away. I look pretty smart, right? But one of those woolly mammoths had to sell it at my purchase price. It's a zero-sum game: I can't win unless some MBA from the Harvard Business School loses.

None of that holds for the individual investor. In fact, it benefits you. The woolly mammoths are the ones who create the short-term happenings. We're the ones making the waters rough in the short run. You're better off looking long term, because if things are generally bad in the packaged food industry, for example, there's nothing I can do about it. Likewise if things are good.

You also have the advantage of speed. As we discussed, I can't sell a lot of stock fast. I can't buy a lot either; the Air Products deal was a rarity, I assure you. When you have an idea that isn't working, you can bail out quickly and start over.

8

Getting Started

A friend hustles toward you in the company cafeteria. He's carrying a tray full of lunch, and he's just busting to sit down and tell you about a great stock tip he just got. The details sound pretty amazing. Company earnings grew 15 percent in the past year. The stock price has doubled. The dividends are up almost as much. This company is doing everything right, your friend tells you, and you'd be a fool not to buy some stock. Then he tells you something else about this amazing company.

It manufactures anvils.

Suddenly, you're not quite as excited about this stock anymore, are you? Something in the back of your mind gives you pause. You can't quite put your finger on it, yet you know this stock isn't such a good idea anymore—whether it's growing at 15 percent or 50 percent a year. Then it dawns on you: Who needs anvils anymore? This story doesn't make any sense. Why would a company that makes anvils be growing like that? We're not living in the Old West. Nobody hammers red-hot iron into horseshoes anymore.

You pass on your friend's hot stock tip. Maybe next time.

If you're interested in stock market investing, that's a good place to start. Change the way you think about everyday life. Open your eyes. Look around you. As I've said, everything in the world is affected by the stock market. Where you shop, where you service your car (and what you drive), what you eat, where you work and play, what clothes you wear—it is all touched by the market somehow. This is one of the key ways you can get started as a stock market investor.

Is your neighborhood department store clean? Are the employees friendly? Does it always have the merchandise you're looking for? Is the parking lot always full of cars? If not, maybe that should tell you something. I once went to Sears looking for some exercise equipment. I wandered around the store for about 15 minutes trying to find what I was looking for and never saw a sales clerk—not one. And I didn't find what I was looking for either. I walked out and found it somewhere else. It confirmed everything I thought I already knew about Sears. It was a crummy company. Their house was not in order. Nobody shopped there. Retailers like Wal-Mart were eating their lunch. I wouldn't have taken Sears stock if they were giving it away. At least, that's how I felt at the time. More on that later.

If you ask those questions and you like the answers, maybe the company is worth investigating as a stock pick. This is how the individual investor can begin to make up for not having eight hours a day to investigate stocks and monitor their progress. Make it a part of your everyday routine. That's important. It will help you past a barrier too few people can break: It will help you buy that first stock. Everyone seems to be interested in the stock market when the economy is strong and the bulls are running. But too many people are paralyzed by thoughts of hibernating bears, cowering in a cave when the market is weak and the economy is bad. You need to adopt a different mind-set: The only way to make money in the stock market is to get in and stay with it.

So how do you start? Once you've opened your eyes to the smorgasbord of stock possibilities in your daily life, what's next?

TRADING PAPER ON PAPER

I recommend minimizing the on-the-job training. While you're learning as much as you can about a range of companies that interest you, you might set up a "paper portfolio" for yourself. Pick 5 or 10 stocks that interest you and "buy" $10,000 worth of each one— or as many as you think you could monitor. Take the prices out of the newspaper every morning and see how your portfolio did each day. For the sake of argument, let's try it with 5 stocks, picked at random from the newspaper. These aren't stock recommendations; they're random picks for the sake of this exercise.

I'll start with 100 shares of Blockbuster Entertainment, the purveyors of video rentals, indoor recreation centers and music stores. Let's add 50 shares of General Motors, 100 shares of The Home Depot, 100 shares of Shawmut National Corp., a northeastern bank, and 100 shares of Wal-Mart. Let's suppose I bought them all at the closing price on October 27, 1993. How much did I spend?

Stock	*#Shares*	*Price/Share*	*Value*
Blockbuster	100	$28.88	$2,888.00
General Motors	50	$46.88	$2,344.00
The Home Depot	100	$38.88	$3,888.00
Shawmut	100	$21.50	$2,155.00
Wal-Mart	100	$25.88	$2,588.00
Total			$13,863.00

We've spent a hefty chunk of change on these stocks, but that's okay. We haven't spent any real money. Remember, this is a paper portfolio. We can act like John D. Rockefeller and spread the cash around any way we want. The idea is to get comfortable with looking up these quotes in the newspaper and seeing how they change from day to day. As time marches on, it will become important to watch the trends in your stock picks and try to figure out what makes the stock price move.

The next day, we open the newspaper again and see how our 5 stocks did on October 28. On the whole, it was a pretty good day; almost all of them went up.

Stock	*#Shares*	*Price/Share*	*Value*
Blockbuster	100	$28.50	$2,850.00
General Motors	50	$49.00	$2,450.00
The Home Depot	100	$39.25	$3,925.00
Shawmut	100	$21.88	$2,188.00
Wal-Mart	100	$26.25	$2,625.00
Total			$14,038.00

In one day, the value of our paper portfolio increased $175—1.3 percent. Only Blockbuster Entertainment dropped. The reason for a $3/8$-point drop in the price on one day may not matter, but you'll pay attention. You'll notice if it happens again (which it did; it lost another $3/8$ the next day) and you'll try to figure out why. You're not investing cash right now. You're investing time. This exercise will make you accustomed to paying attention to the news that affects your stock picks. What does the company do? Who is buying their products, and how much? What decisions is management making? Is management changing?

As you're assembling your paper portfolio, here are a few things to keep in mind. These apply whether you're investing Monopoly money or cold, hard cash. And later, we'll spend more time assembling a paper portfolio and tracking some of the stats and stocks.

DIVERSIFY

Stocks are risky investments. Antique rocking chairs are risky investments too. CDs are risky in their own way—you're putting opportunity on the line. You need to spread the risk around and buying stock in five different companies—like we did in our example above—isn't very diverse. On the other hand, if you have 100 different stocks, chances are pretty good that you won't do much worse than the stock market as a whole. That's not entirely bad. The stock market has an upward bias. In other words, it tends to rise.

Realistically, few individual investors are inclined to buy shares in 100 different companies. I think 10 is a good number—but it's an absolute minimum number. If you buy more than that, 20 different companies in different industries, I consider that even better.

REMEMBER THE FARMER AND THE BUSINESSMAN?

They didn't know what to buy, they only knew what not to buy. When you pick those 20 stocks, you need to be able to explain why you bought them. It wouldn't hurt to write down why you bought what you bought. My colleagues do. I have loose-leaf binders full of stock recommendations like this: "Home Depot is doing very well. Earnings were up 88.3 percent in fiscal year 1988 and earnings are projected to be up another 33 percent to $1.50 in fiscal year 1989. Sales are up in excess of 20 percent so far and the company has announced a move into the northeast which has the oldest (and therefore the most in need of repair) housing market in the United States."

These sheets include numbers. What were the earnings per share last year? What are the projected earnings next year? Earnings per share are the engine that drive stock market investing. A company that's not making money—more and more money every year—isn't growing. That money is reflected in earnings per share.

Buy Stock in Companies You Understand

It's a related point to the farmer and businessman, but it's a point worth making. If you've got a compelling stock idea, you ought to be able to explain why it's so good in three or four minutes. That means that if you buy stock in an electric utility, you presumably understand how your state's public utility commission operates, how the commissioners and the company arrive at rate decisions, what those decisions mean for the company and how they fit into the statewide picture. Retailing is simple. Maybe that's why many of my stock choices have focused on that segment of the economy. What could be more simple to understand than the retail industry? Companies like Wal-Mart, The Gap and Toys "R" Us put stuff on their shelves and you buy it. A company called PetSmart intends to be the "category killer" of pet supplies. It is a huge superstore filled with rawhide bones, plastic water dishes, grooming supplies, pet food, toys—everything you can imagine a pet would need and a few things you wouldn't. I just need to decide if this company is well managed and well positioned to make a killing. And, of course, whether the stock is cheap.

Sounds like a simple idea, right? You'd be surprised how many investors buy stock in rocket research, chemical companies and software manufacturers with no inkling of how any of those industries operate or, for that matter, what those companies do.

What's Your Style?

I bought my first house in 1971, a $41,000, three-bedroom in Glen Ellyn, Illinois. Before I bought it, I plotted out my strategy for house hunting.

First, I decided I wanted to be able to ride the train to work in Oak Park, so I investigated every town along the line and settled on Glen Ellyn as the one for me. Then, I decided I wanted to live close enough to the train station to walk there each morning and home each evening. I didn't want my walk to be more than a mile, so I got a map of the town and drew a box that encompassed every neighborhood within a mile of the station. I drove up and down the streets within that box and highlighted every street I liked with red ink. I was ready to start looking.

When a house went on the market and I saw it advertised in the paper, I could readily rule it out if it didn't fall within my box on a red street. In a few weeks, I got to know the city quite well and the houses within my parameters even better. By the first week of April that year, I started noticing the houses that had been on the market were selling pretty quickly. I knew the bear market was over, so I stepped up my search, moved in and found the house I wanted.

That's my style, the way I do business. I have a plan, a strategy. I prepare myself by learning everything I can about whatever I'm doing. I'm knowledgable enough to make my move when the opportunity opens up.

What's your style?

You need one. You need some method to your madness before you start buying stocks. The most successful investors have a philosophy, a few key guidelines to follow as they're making their stock picks, *and they stick with that method through thick and thin.* Investors who change their minds every week about the kinds of stocks they buy, how long they hold them or what they expect from them are destined for rough seas—and large losses.

I've been described in numerous newspaper and magazine articles something like this: A lover of large companies; a hater of companies with high debt; a rapid trader, who turns over 100 percent of his portfolio each year; a lover of rapid (but not too rapid) growth, who expects to see earnings-per-share increase at around 15 percent a year.

This is me. It doesn't have to be you.

The range of investment styles is large, but every style has a single question at its core: How much risk can you stomach?

I've said it before, you've heard it over and over, but it still bears repeating: There is no such thing as a no-risk investment. Even if you stuff your paycheck in a cookie jar, you risk losing out on potential growth with other investments or losing buying power as inflation whittles away at your savings. I will grant you this: The chance of losing your principal is pretty low with the cookie-jar technique. If you want to do better than even, however, you need to decide how much you're willing to risk the principal.

On that subject, risk runs from zero to infinity. You could put all your money into government treasury bills or government-guaranteed certificates of deposit. You won't risk a cent of your principal—except what is eroded by inflation. You could work up the range through corporate bonds, high-dividend paying stocks, emerging growth stocks, penny stocks, junk bonds, options. There are investments that are so risky, you might as well just throw your money out the window—if only they didn't tempt us with such high potential returns.

My advice: Stick to the middle ground. Certificates of deposit and treasury bills aren't investments. Not in my book, anyway. Options are too far out of the ballpark. Oh, they are investments, and we will discuss them in more detail later, but who has the time or the expertise to make them work? Not me. Besides, I'm sticking with the stats that say stocks do better than any other investment over the long haul.

So what kind of stock market investor can you be? Again, there's a range of risk, even in the stock market. Some companies are inherently more risky, but they offer the chance of higher returns because they are small and emerging. Others are large, lumbering companies that offer lackluster growth potential but steady, reliable dividend income. Let's work our way up the risk/reward range and talk about the kinds of companies you might look at in each category—and what kind of investor likes them. These categories are broad, but you'll get the idea (see Figure 8-1).

The Income Investor. Typically, this investor is older and more conservative, seeking income to supplement a pension and Social Security and savings. This type has some principal but doesn't have a lot of interest in risking it. Frankly, those are the *only* investors who ought to be thinking about investing solely for income. Anyone with some cash and youth can probably get better returns with another style. Still, some income investors do very well because some low-expectation stocks exceed those expectations.

What's Your Style?

These are broad areas. Which one are you closest to?

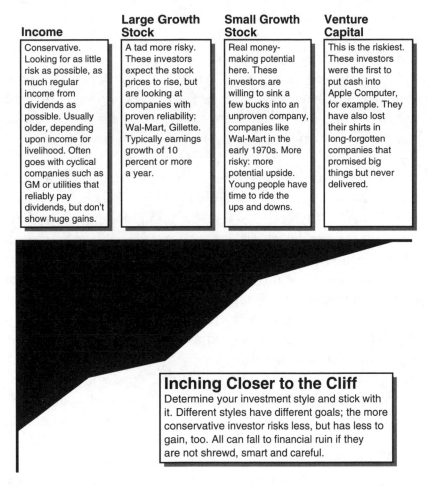

Income	Large Growth Stock	Small Growth Stock	Venture Capital
Conservative. Looking for as little risk as possible, as much regular income from dividends as possible. Usually older, depending upon income for livelihood. Often goes with cyclical companies such as GM or utilities that reliably pay dividends, but don't show huge gains.	A tad more risky. These investors expect the stock prices to rise, but are looking at companies with proven reliability: Wal-Mart, Gillette. Typically earnings growth of 10 percent or more a year.	Real money-making potential here. These investors are willing to sink a few bucks into an unproven company, companies like Wal-Mart in the early 1970s. More risky: more potential upside. Young people have time to ride the ups and downs.	This is the riskiest. These investors were the first to put cash into Apple Computer, for example. They have also lost their shirts in long-forgotten companies that promised big things but never delivered.

Inching Closer to the Cliff
Determine your investment style and stick with it. Different styles have different goals; the more conservative investor risks less, but has less to gain, too. All can fall to financial ruin if they are not shrewd, smart and careful.

Fig. 8-1

Income investors are looking for solid, strong, reliable companies that pay quarterly dividends. In other words, they divide some of their profits among the company's stockholders—anywhere from a few pennies per share to several dollars per share. Cyclical companies such as General Motors, which see their stocks react to the cycle of the economy, typically pay dividends that income investors seek. So do utility companies. These investors aren't looking for their investment capital to grow. Their money is in the stock because it stakes their claim to a piece of the company's future earnings. You're not likely to see enormous changes in the stock price, but these investors expect to see dividends rising modestly every year.

Large Growth Stock Investors. This type takes a tad more risk than income investors. Remember, income investors don't expect much growth in their investment capital. Here, you do. You want to see earnings rise every year, you'd like to see the stock price rise. You want the underlying value of your assets to continue to increase. You want a Wal-Mart or a Gillette, a large company with an established track record with earnings growth of more than 10 percent a year.

Small Growth Stock Investors: Now we're talking some real money-making potential. Let's suppose you bought stock in Wal-Mart in the 1970s, when it was a small company and most of the shareholders were the folks in Arkansas. You'd have seen your stock increase a hundredfold since then. But who would have known? How could you know this small department store in the middle of a tiny southern state was going to sweep the country? You didn't, of course. You took a bigger risk, and you made a bigger bundle similar to The Home Depot in the mid-1980s. Here in the early 1990s, you might be doing the same thing with a Cott, which manufactures private label soft drinks, or Office Depot, the white-collar version of The Home Depot, its warehouse-style shelves piled high with computer equipment, paper, pens, desk accessories and paper clips.

Clearly, the difference between large- and small-growth investing is that the larger companies have been growth stories for years. You figure they have a much greater chance of continuing; the smaller companies are more risky because they haven't been tested. You don't know what will happen when things are bad. But the small stocks grow faster than the big stocks—and they have further to grow, more upside. There is greater risk but potentialy greater reward. Of course, you can go even further.

Venture Capital Investors. A lot of technology stocks fall into this category. Here's the pitch: "I've got a great new product, something nobody in the world has ever seen before. It could be a dud. Maybe nobody will buy it. Maybe all this time and money and effort will have been wasted. But maybe, just maybe, this will be the next Apple computer, compact disc player, hand-held camcorder. . . ." You'll never know unless you try—and unless you're willing to put your money on the line.

Me, I'm more of a large- to medium-growth investor, but I can be tempted on most anything. You just evolve. And you can change as you learn more about your strengths and weaknesses in investing, as long as you do it carefully. As a rule, it's not a good idea to change your investing pattern or the type of stocks you buy in the same way you change your underwear. There will always be times when your style of investing is in favor and times when it will be out of favor. If you attempt to predict when those times have changed and to adjust your style to those changes, then you'll almost certainly fail. You'll be doing what you're not good at, and you'll be competing with people who are good at it.

Whatever style you prefer, pick one and stick with it. The worst style to pick is the market timer. He buys when he thinks the market is rising and sells everything when the market looks bad. Sounds reasonable, but it's very tough to do. Would you like to see how a market timer loses and a consistent investor wins? (see Figure 8-2) If that graph doesn't make my argument perfectly clear, then nothing will.

FINDING A BROKER

A stockbroker that provides investment advice isn't necessary to becoming a successful investor—I don't have one. However, a good one can help you to develop an investment strategy, monitor the progress of the companies you choose and alert you when a change is due. A broker will want to know how much money you have to invest, how much debt you're carrying and something about the kinds of companies you're interested in to help you decide what your investment strategy will be.

The Risk of Timing the Market

Market timers put their money into the stock market when things start to look good, then yank it when things look bad. That means they miss some of the best trading days. This graph shows your annual rate of return if you had never left the market between 1983 and 1992—and the consequences when you miss the best trading days.

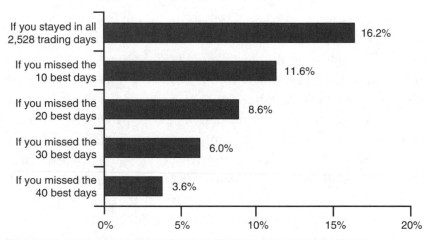

If you stayed in all
2,528 trading days — 16.2%

If you missed the
10 best days — 11.6%

If you missed the
20 best days — 8.6%

If you missed the
30 best days — 6.0%

If you missed the
40 best days — 3.6%

0%   5%   10%   15%   20%

Figures assume assets not invested in the market were earning interest at the average rate of 30-year Treasury bills from 1983-93.

Fig. 8-2 Source: Datastream, Ibbottson Assoc. and Sanford C. Berstein & Co.

In other words, you need to reread the last section and to decide on a style before you start hunting for a broker. You need to have some convictions about what you're willing to do with your money—then make those convictions clear to your broker. You must tell him or her what you expect out of any investment program, for example: "Inflation is 3 percent, bonds are yielding 7 percent and I would like stocks that pay, on average, at least 3 percent but give me 7 percent in appreciation. I don't want to do options, I don't want wild and crazy things, I don't want to speculate."

Or you could say, "I just came into all this money, and I'm young and want aggressive growth stocks; I don't care about income; I don't need it." Both objectives are fine if you're the right person.

You will, of course, want to know a few things about your broker before you start doing business. Picking a broker is not unlike picking an accountant, a doctor or a lawyer: Who do your friends recommend and why? There are a lot of lousy brokers out there; a lot of the bad ones know that the only way they make money is for you to buy or sell stock. They make a commission on every transaction, so if they're recommending that you buy one stock or sell another, you need to have the confidence that your broker has your best interest at heart, not his or hers.

INSIDE LINE

Don't rely on Wall Street, your broker or a stock market analyst to tell you when you should sell. Most investment people are poor sellers. Why? An analyst who covers a particular industry depends on access to the companies within that industry for information. A sell recommendation doesn't make their sources of information very happy. For the broker, a sell recommendation means admitting a mistake—and nobody likes to do that.

Besides, by the time your broker's firm issues a sell recommendation, the mere recommendation can make the stock price fall—and you miss the peak price. You need to develop your own discipline about when to buy or sell.

That will be one of your first questions: What's the turnover in your broker's typical account? What stocks does the broker like and why? What kind of research does your broker do on his or her own? What would make your broker telephone you with information?

All this advice is good, common sense—the broker, the philosophy, the stocks you understand—but none of it matters unless you're making the big decisions. You have to step up to the bar and buy. You can't wait for all the good news on your favorite stock to roll in. You need to buy before that happens; by the time all the good news comes in, everyone else has acted on it and the price will be out of your reach. It's too easy to talk yourself out of doing anything. Nobody wants to look dumb. The stock market is all about making someone else look dumb. Any time you buy a stock, you're saying your perception of that stock is right and the other person is wrong. And that's really all it is.

Sears Becomes Solid Again

I said in the last chapter that at the time I wouldn't take Sears stock if they were giving it away. And that was true—at the time. But in the two years since I started this project, my opinion of the company has changed, mostly because the company knew it was having problems (how could they not?) and worked to fix them.

Between late 1991 and early 1994, Sears turned itself around. I actually owned some stock in the company by the time this book was finished. The company's sales were better than most other retailers—in fact, they were among the best in the industry. After 20 years of languishing in the bottom of the retail industry, lumbering under the weight of all its diversity (and its image), the company finally got some management at the top that was prepared to make tough decisions. They closed the catalog business, which had lost money for years. They sold or spun off some of the company's subsidiaries. They renovated and upgraded many of their aging stores. They created a niche market with their "Sears Brand Central" appliance stores.

I bought my first Sears stock in years in October 1993. I'm still waiting to see how it does and whether I'm happy with the investment.

You must continue to follow companies, even when you don't like them. If a company continues to do poorly year after year after year, it will go bankrupt. It won't be your problem anymore. If it doesn't go bankrupt, you must assume that someday, it could become a favored stock again. You want to be ready if and when it happens.

9

What's It Worth to You?

If you've ever listened to investors talking about the stock market, you might mistake the subject of their conversation for an angry child, a scorned lover or a wise prophet. Wall Street discussions often concern themselves with "what the market did" today or "how the market reacted" to something. The market "tells" us about the state of the economy. The market is "ready" for good news or it is "preparing" for a correction. All this seems to roll off of our tongues as though the stock exchange had a mind of its own, and all of us were just servants at its beck and call.

Funny thing is, it's amazing how often the market is right, and people just aren't paying attention to what it is saying. In my office, if one of our stock holdings is dropping every day, its share price slipping further down, then I'll call an analyst and ask, "What's wrong?" Nine times out of ten, the analyst will say there's nothing wrong. They'll hold their ground and come up with some lame explanation—more sellers than buyers, perhaps. My stock answer is usually just as simple: You don't know what you're talking about. Dig harder. Find something. Of course, if there is no reason, then a buying opportunity is at hand. You can, of course, reverse the

85

example with a stock that keeps going up. If no reason can be found for this, start selling some. If it goes higher, sell more.

In either case, the market is trying to tell you something. If you don't act, you're not listening.

Analysts don't like to be told they don't know what they're talking about. Essentially, I'm telling them that they haven't done their homework and that they don't know how to analyze a stock. But when the market tells you something is wrong, you ought to find out what the problem is. Nobody sells down the price of a stock because everything is fine. The reason they sell their stock may be faulty, but there is a reason. And it's possible the answer won't concern you. You may want to continue holding that stock—even buy more. But you can't make that decision until you know what the market is saying.

The stock market talks to us almost nonstop throughout the day, a rambling monolog of numbers and ticker symbols, volumes, prices, percentages and ratios. The easiest way to catch up, of course, is to pick up the business section of your paper every morning and find your stocks in the stock tables. We've compared them to baseball box scores already; now let's think of them as the stock market's daily mouthpiece.

Let's pick a stock at random and discuss what the stock tables can tell us about it every day (for a summary, see Figure 9-1).

Reading the Stock Tables

This is torn out of The Wall Street Journal, showing stock listings for Friday, September 23, 1994. We'll take a look at the key numbers for McDonald's, one of the 30 stocks in the Dow Jones Industrial Average.

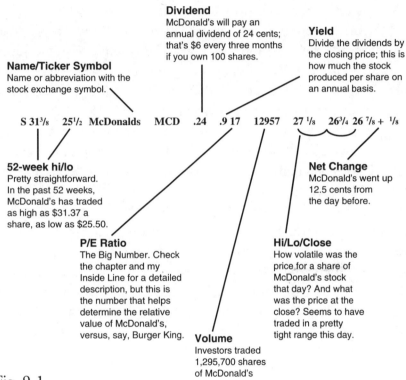

Dividend
McDonald's will pay an annual dividend of 24 cents; that's $6 every three months if you own 100 shares.

Yield
Divide the dividends by the closing price; this is how much the stock produced per share on an annual basis.

Name/Ticker Symbol
Name or abbreviation with the stock exchange symbol.

S 31³/₈   25¹/₂ McDonalds   MCD   .24   .9 17   12957   27 ¹/₈   26³/₄ 26 ⁷/₈ + ¹/₈

52-week hi/lo
Pretty straightforward. In the past 52 weeks, McDonald's has traded as high as $31.37 a share, as low as $25.50.

Net Change
McDonald's went up 12.5 cents from the day before.

P/E Ratio
The Big Number. Check the chapter and my Inside Line for a detailed description, but this is the number that helps determine the relative value of McDonald's, versus, say, Burger King.

Hi/Lo/Close
How volatile was the price for a share of McDonald's stock that day? And what was the price at the close? Seems to have traded in a pretty tight range this day.

Volume
Investors traded 1,295,700 shares of McDonald's

Fig. 9-1

52-wk				Yld							
hi	lo	Stock	sym	%	div	PE	100s	hi	lo	last	chg
49¹/₄	32³/₄	Goodyear	GT	1.3	.60	14	1302	47⁷/₈	45⁵/₈	46⁵/₈	+³/₄

We'll run through some of these items rather quickly. There is only one number among them that I want to spend some time discussing.

First of all, this information comes from the stock pages of a local Florida newspaper, but it is very similiar to what you'd get each day in *The Wall Street Journal*, which has as comprehensive a stock table as you'll need. A lot of local newspapers run stock tables, but may not include all the information found in the *WSJ*. That may be fine for you; maybe you won't need that much information. However, it's good to know where to get it if you want it.

At the far left, you see a couple of numbers right off the bat, and let's take the time to notice that we're talking about Goodyear Tire and Rubber Co., a company that anyone who has owned a car or has seen their blimp at a football game recognizes. You can find the company's ticker symbol next to the name.

The 52-week high and low price tells investors a little something about how volatile Goodyear stock has been in the prior year. Its price has been as high as $49.25 a share and as low as $32.75 a share during that period.

Next to the ticker symbol, you can find the company's per-share dividend, the annual amount the company will pay from its profits to its shareholders. If you own 100 shares of Goodyear, then you'll stand to get $60 in quarterly payments of $15. The next column is related, showing the annual yield of the stock based on its closing share price that day and its dividend. Divide the dividend ($.60) by the closing price at the far right end of the listing ($46 $^{5}/_{8}$) and you should come up with about 0.0128, or nearly 1.3 percent.

At the far right, we see that Goodyear's price changed from the day before. It closed at $46.62 a share on this day and $.75 higher than the day before. Working our way in from the right now, we can see the high and low prices for the day, another indication of how volatile the price can be during a one-day period. In this case, it changed about $1.12 during the course of the day. The volume traded is simply how many shares changed hands that day— 130 +$^{3}/_{4}$.

That leaves one more number in that hodgepodge page of stock stats. We'll spend the rest of this chapter talking about it and the rest of the book referring to it. For my way of doing business, the "price/earnings" ratio (p/e) is one of the most important numbers in the bunch. Why? Because that's the number that helps me determine how much a stock is worth compared with similar stocks in the industry or to the stock market as a whole. I use the p/e ratio as a measure of value: How much is ABC Widget stock worth? I may know what ABC's stock is selling for, but that doesn't necessarily tell me how cheap it is. Let's put it this way: I have paid $79 a share for Procter & Gamble and considered it a bargain, but I have passed up The Home Depot at $50 a share because I considered it too expensive.

For example, suppose I know that you earn $15,000 a year working for a particular company. In a vacuum of information, that doesn't tell me much about what you do and how valuable you are to your company. But if I have a benchmark to compare your salary against—an average salary, for example—then I have a point of reference. If the average salary at your firm is $25,000, then that tells me you're a lot lower on the totem pole than somebody who brings down $50,000 a year.

In a similar way, the p/e ratio creates benchmarks that give investors a point of reference for their stock picks, a way to compare how one stock is doing next to another (or next to the market as a whole).

So how do you figure the p/e ratio? When our simple stock page tells us Goodyear has a p/e ratio of 14, what does that mean? Important questions, of course, but we'll have to stop here for a short side trip before we get back aboard the main line. We'll abandon Goodyear for the sake of this discussion.

The p/e ratio—just like miles per hour and revolutions per minute—shows the relationship between two numbers. In this case, the ratio is the share price of a particular company divided by the company's earnings per share. Before that means anything, you need to understand the importance of earnings (the common shorthand for "earnings per share") to stock market investors.

Let's just be blunt about it: Investors and corporations live and die by the earnings estimate. Whole squadrons of analysts are holed up in their Wall Street offices making a living by reading balance sheets, scanning annual reports, interviewing chief financial officers, sizing up competitors and, ultimately, deciding how much a particular company is going to earn in the next 3 months, 6 months, 12 months, 5 years. The estimates are probably more important to investors than the current, actual earnings numbers. The current earnings per share can be distorted by writeoffs, strikes, accounting changes and so forth. Besides, the past is done. Investors prefer earnings estimates, generally for the next 12–18 months. They show the outlook for the company. Is it going to make money? And are those earnings going to continue to rise? Investors want to know what's going to happen in the future more than what has already happened. At the same time, Wall Street doesn't like surprises. If Wall Street expects one number and gets another (lower) one, then nobody is happy. Reducing a company's earnings estimate once is bad; reducing it twice is the kiss of death.

Watch the papers: The next time a major corporation shows poorer-than-expected earnings, see what happens to the stock price. It's similar to the swallows returning to Capistrano. You know exactly what's going to happen before it happens.

From this discussion, I'm sure you have inferred that earnings are a significant number to track whenever you make a stock pick. This number is the one that investors are referring to when they say a company has "grown" 15 percent year over year. They are really interested in how much a company's earnings per share have grown. You'll want to see what a company's historical growth has been and what analysts expect to happen to that growth. If earnings have not risen year after year and if they are not expected to continue rising, then what's the point? There isn't a corporation in America that doesn't have the same goal: making money. A company that doesn't see its earnings rise over time is simply withering on the vine.

Now we can get back on track. Because you now have an idea about how important earnings are, you probably have a hint about how important (in my view) the p/e ratio is.

Let's look at our favorite fictional corporation again, the ABC Widget Co. Let's cast ABC in the role of a wildly popular, extremely successful company. Let us also make the math very simple: ABC sells at $100 a share on the New York Stock Exchange and posts earnings of $5 a share. Simple division: 100 divided by 5 equals 20. That's the p/e ratio for ABC Widget.

That number tells you how much investors are willing to pay for every dollar of ABC's earnings. When you buy a stock, you're essentially buying a stream of earnings, placing a bet on how well you expect a company to make money in the future. Still, even that number doesn't tell you much unless you have a similar number to place next to it. In a sense, that's the beauty of the p/e ratio. Although it might not let you compare apples to oranges, it does at least let investors compare Macintosh apples with Golden Delicious apples.

You should be able to find out the p/e ratio of the market as a whole in either your own newspaper listings or *The Wall Street Journal.* The principle is the same: Divide the market's aggregate earnings into its aggregate share price as represented by the Standard & Poor's 500 index. Suppose we did that and found the market's p/e ratio to be 15. That starts to tell us something about ABC Widget's value. For one, it says investors are willing to pay more for ABC's earnings than they are for the market as a whole—a 33 percent premium to the market, in fact. It looks like ABC is in an industry that people like, where people see potential. In a sense, that premium value says, "This is a stock people value more highly than most others." Either that or the $5 in earnings is considered well below what people feel the company *could* earn in the next year or two. In other words, investors might be saying, "Sure, I'll pay a few extra bucks *now* for those $5 in earnings. But I think earnings are going to go up. As the earnings go up, the price I paid now will become a bargain."

Suppose ABC's p/e ratio was lower than the market's—a 10 versus the market's 15. What does that tell us? Now we can say ABC is selling at a 33 percent discount to the market. ABC is "cheap" relative to the market as a whole. People are not willing to pay as much for ABC's earnings. Why? There could be several reasons.

Maybe the widget industry as a whole is struggling because the economy has forced customers to cut back their widget inventory. Perhaps only ABC is having troubles because of poor management or some other unique situation. Or maybe, just maybe, the omnipotent, all-seeing "market" misperceives the value of ABC's stock. Your goal is to find those companies, the ones that you think could be worth more. And you will always be looking for why you think a company could be worth more than it already is. Maybe it has some hidden, unrealized value, such as a drug company that has a groundbreaking drug awaiting approval.

It is overly simplistic to take this one number—the p/e ratio—and annoint it with mystical powers that will point you to that mythical diamond in a salt mine. It is simply a tool, another way the stock market "tells" us what it knows. And while there are reasons it is valuable to compare a stock's p/e ratio to the market as a whole, it is also valuable to hold it up against the p/e ratio of a comparable company. I do it all the time. It's my bread and butter, one of the first things I want to know before I sell one stock and buy a competitor's.

We'll go through a realistic example of how I use the p/e ratio in just a moment, but first, remember these steps for making the p/e ratio relevent:

1. Compare one company's p/e ratio to the p/e of the entire market. I usually express this as a percentage (i.e., ABC's p/e is 133 percent of the market's).

2. Make the same calculation with a comparable company (i.e., XYZ Cog's p/e is 124 percent of the market's).

3. Learn the trading history of the companies you're interested in. That way, you'll know when a company's p/e ratio is relatively high or relatively low against its historical range. Again, more on this in a minute.

4. Be aware of situations when one company is peaking and another might be dropping.

I use these techniques all the time, comparing one company with another and using the p/e ratios to help judge when one company's stock is cheap and another company's is expensive. I call this technique "pairs trading." The pairs could be pairs of anything: drug companies, retailers, food stores, auto companies. I wouldn't pair up The Limited clothing stores and General Motors; they are fundamentally different companies. I would consider pairing up The Limited and The Gap, however, because they are similar and because—all things being equal—I wouldn't expect their prices to be out of line with each other. One should be as much a bargain (or as bad) as the other. Of course, all things are never equal. So how do you determine when one's a bargain and one's a rip-off?

Well, to start with, I have spent a lot of time watching these two companies. I know what makes them perform well or struggle; I have seen where their stock price performs historically. I also know what their earnings have historically been. Therefore, I also know what I can expect their p/e ratios to be relative to each other. In simple English, I know the range in which I can *usually* find The Limited's p/e ratio, and I know the *usual* range of The Gap's p/e ratio. Remember that. It's important. And take heart: These things will become second nature as you identify companies that are interesting to you as an investor.

Now, let's get to the example I was referring to. In late 1990, my staff and I took another look at those two retailers and made an investment decision based, in this case, largely on the p/e ratios we saw.

The Limited and The Gap fall well within my criteria for picking out an investment: Both are retailers, something I understand very well. You sell something, I buy it. Simple. Both have been well-managed companies, both were growing between 15 percent and 20 percent a year. And both are similar enough that they could fall together in my "pairs trading" scheme.

At the time we took another look at the two companies, we sized up the numbers and wrote down a few details about both companies in a recommendation sheet, something we routinely keep on companies we watch (see Figure 9-2).

Fig. 9-2

Limited, Inc.
Gap, Inc.

Date: 11/19/90

			-EPS-		-p/e-		p/e relative to S&P 400			
	Price	Range	1990	1991	1990	1991	1990	1991	Div.	Yield
GSP	$30.62	$35-19	$1.85	$2.05	16.6	14.9	1.12	1.03x	$0.05	1.7%
LTD	14.50	25-12	1.10	1.25	13.2	11.6	.90	.80	0.24	1.7%
S&P	370.14		25.50	25.00	14.8	14.5	1.00	1.00	12.30	3.3%

	GPS	LTD
Recommendation:	Sell	Buy
Est. p/e range:	90-115%	80-105%
Downside/upside (12 mo.)	$26-34	$14-19
Ave. Daily trading (NYSE)	300,000	900,000

I. Business

   Limited, Inc. (LTD) and Gap, Inc. (GPS) are both specialty apparel retailers. GPS sells primarily casual wear to
both men and women and LTD sells a more fashion forward look
almost exclusively to women.

   GPS and LTD have traveled separate paths this year. GPS
is having a record year and surpassing all expectations. LTD,
on the other hand, while having a record year, is not meeting
either investors' expectations or their own. Both stories
are well known. GPS's basic casual wear is going over very
well and appealing to an ever-wider public (even selling to
the over-50 crowd), GAP Kids is doing well and
Banana Republic is turning around after two years of hard
times. LTD is having problems in The Limited, Limited Express and Lerners. So while GPS's earnings per share should
increase from $1.49 to $1.85-$1.90 (24%), LTD's eps will only
increase from $0.96 to $1.10 (15%).

Looked at another way, though, LTD is doing very well under pretty bad conditions. The Limited accounts for about 50% of sales and about the same in profits and its comps (comparable store sales) have been negative for about six months. The prime reason for this was the failure of the "Paul DuFrier" line, introduced last spring. Management realized they had a flop within weeks and ordered new designs and cut planned buying of the old designs. Recently, newer merchandise has come in and sales trends are better. Limited Express's problems were limited to the third quarter and seemed to be due to the lack of inventory because of cautious buying. Here again, recent trends are encouraging. Finally, Lerners is going through its third turnaround in about four years. Maybe they will get it right this time, but if they don't it won't matter because profitability is already very low.

We believe that a switch is in order between GPS and LTD. LTD is selling at the bottom of its range and GPS is at the top of theirs. Yet there isn't that much different between the two. Both will grow at about 15-20%, have good managements, and are among the best at what they do. Thus a 22% difference in their p/e's seems excessive. We recommend a swap.

II. Valuation:

We think that GPS can sell between 90% to 115% of the market while LTD can sell between 80% and 105%. With GPS at the top of its range and LTD at the bottom of its, we recommend a switch.

Here's what it told us, step by step:

- For 1990, The Gap's earnings per share would be $1.85, up about 20 percent for the year. For The Limited, earnings were going to rise to about $1.10 a share, or about 15 percent. Both respectable.

- For 1991, we expected earnings to be $2.05 for The Gap and $1.25 for The Limited.

- Take the stock price for The Gap on this particular day and divide it by The Gap's earnings per share: $30.62 a share, divided by $1.85 equals a p/e ratio of 16.6 in 1990. In 1991, using that year's expected earnings, the p/e would be 14.9.

- Do the same for The Limited: $14.50 a share, divided by $1.10 in earnings equals a p/e ratio of 13.2. In 1991, using that year's expected earnings, the p/e would be 11.6.

In sumary, this means The Gap's p/e was expected to be about 16.6 in 1990 (about 112 percent of the market) and 14.9 in 1991 (about 103 percent of the market). The Limited's p/e was expected to be 13.2 (or 90 percent of the market p/e) in 1990 and 11.6 (or 80 percent of the market) in 1991.

We have just accomplished steps 1 and 2 that I mentioned earlier. So what does it mean so far?

In The Gap's case, it means investors love this company, relative to the market as a whole. With a p/e ratio at 112 percent of the market's p/e, it is selling at a premium. A dollar's worth of The Gap's earnings is selling for 12 percent more than a dollar's worth of earnings marketwide. In The Limited's case, the company is selling at a discount to the market. A dollar's worth of The Limited's earnings costs only 90 percent of the average marketwide.

Still, this story isn't complete until we move to step 3: Learn the trading history of the companies you're interested in.

If you've checked Figure 9-2, then you've noticed that The Limited's p/e ratio is typically between 80 percent and 105 percent of the market p/e. The Gap, meanwhile, usually has a p/e between 90 percent and 115 percent of the market's. Now we have all the elements.

In my recommendation sheet, I note that The Gap's p/e should be at 112 percent of the market's—near the top of its range. Meanwhile, The Limited's p/e will be at about 90 percent of the market's, falling to 80 percent—the bottom of its range.

To me, that suggests that the Gap has less "upside." Investors aren't going to be willing to pay much more for The Gap based on its history. The Gap's price looks expensive. But look at The Limited: There is nothing wrong with this company, yet its p/e ratio is low. It has more "upside."

Why do I say that?

Mathematically, there are only two ways the p/e ratio can rise: One way would be for the earnings to go down. If that happens, then we've already discussed the calamity it would be. The p/e ratio also can rise if the stock price goes up. So if a company's p/e ratio is at its low end and you don't see anything else wrong with it, then that suggests the price is cheap. It could rise again.

So what did I write on the recommendation sheet? "We believe that a switch is in order between The Gap and The Limited. The Limited is selling at the bottom of its range and The Gap is at the top. Yet there isn't that much difference between the two. Both will grow at about 15 percent to 20 percent, have good managements and are among the best at what they do. Thus, a 22 percent difference in the p/es seems excessive."

Based on my knowledge of the two companies and my understanding of the p/e ratio, I decided, quite simply, that The Gap's price was too expensive and possibly due for a small tumble and that The Limited's price was ripe for a rise. Guess what? I was mostly right: Two months later, The Limited's stock price jumped 30 percent to $18.87. Meanwhile, The Gap's price rose only 9 percent—not a lot, but obviously we missed the peak with The Gap. At that point, we revised our expectations for The Gap and decided its p/e could fall between 90 percent and 120 percent of the market's. We decided to buy both stocks for a while.

The toughest part about comparing one company's p/e ratio (and its range) to the market's, however, is realizing that everything can change very quickly. Not only is the price of your company changing day to day—and, therefore, its p/e ratio—so is the aggregate price of the market and *its* p/e ratio. Let's concentrate on The Gap for a minute so you see what I mean.

On January 17, 1991, only 10 days after deciding to buy The Gap's stock again, we noticed it had gone up 22.4 percent. Great move! We decided it was already time to take the money and run. The Gap's price of $41, divided by its revised earnings of $1.95 per share produced a p/e of 21—137 percent of the market's p/e at the time! That was well above where we believed it could go.

Sell, we said.

Three weeks later, the aggregate price of the Standard & Poor's 400 had climbed nearly 10 percent while The Gap was up only 7 percent. That means the market's p/e ratio went up faster than The Gap's. If the difference had been more extreme, you can see what could happen: The Gap's p/e relative to the market might no longer be at the high end of its range. I'll show you what I mean, but for the sake of argument, let's suppose the market had gone up 25 percent and The Gap hadn't gone up at all. Here's what the numbers would be:

The market would be selling at an aggregate price of $479.65. With earnings of $25 a share, the market's p/e would be 19.2. The Gap would still have a price of $41, earnings of $1.95 and a p/e of 21. That means that suddenly, without a single change in The Gap, the company's p/e is 109 percent of the market's— neither cheap nor expensive. You can see it gets complicated. Nobody said it was easy.

Now let's get back to both companies with another hypothetical example. When first we met these two clothing retailers, The Gap looked expensive and The Limited looked cheap, remember?

Suppose a few weeks pass and The Limited's price goes up 20 percent while The Gap remain's flat. Suddenly, The Limited has a much higher p/e ratio and no longer looks so cheap.

Why? Let's do the math. The Limited's earnings haven't changed any since the stock price went up. It was earning $1.10 a share. Within the month, suppose its stock price rose from $14.50 a share to $17.40 a share—20 percent. That means its p/e ratio (price divided by earnings) went from 13.2 to 15.8. When you compare that with the S&P's, The Limited's p/e is no longer 90 percent of the market, but 107 percent of the market. Suddenly, The Limited's p/e ratio is above expectations for the *high end of its range.* At the same time, The Gap's p/e ratio hasn't changed because its earnings and its share price have remained flat.

Now, as an investor, I'm curious. The market is telling me that The Limited is more valuable because other investors are willing to pay more for each dollar of the company's earnings. Meanwhile, investors are not that interested in The Gap. Its value hasn't increased. Another way to say it: The Limited is more expensive than The Gap. Its stock is selling at *more of a premium* than The Gap's. Think of it as two cans of soup on the grocery store shelf. One sells for $.89; another sells for $1.25. Do you automatically assume the more expensive one is better?

Of course not. We won't do that with these two stocks either. We look at the "fundamentals" of both companies. Has management changed? Does either one have excessive inventory? Are they involved in major litigation? Is there any *fundamental* reason why The Limited would suddenly get so out of line? Is there any *fundamental* reason why The Gap could not see growth? If the answer to both those questions is no, then maybe it's the right time to sell the "expensive" Limited stock, which looks as though its price has risen out of line. Maybe it's time to buy the "cheaper" Gap stock.

This example is made up, obviously, but these examples happen all the time. It should begin to show how I compare one stock against another to determine which ones look like the good buys. Read the recommendation in Figure 9-2 closely for an idea of how "intangibles" like clothing design play into the formula.

And remember: The p/e measures how much the market is willing to pay for each dollar of earnings. Typically, when outlooks are good, p/e ratios are high. The p/e rises when investors are optimistic about a company's current and future earnings. The hackneyed old saw about investing in the stock market told us to "Buy low, sell high." Well this chapter should show us that it's a little more complicated than that. You need to know how to tell what's low and what's high. Instead, we should advise, "Buy cheap, sell expensive."

More about the P/E Ratio

You're browsing in the meat section at the supermarket, and you notice a package of chicken selling for $1.49 a pound. You pick it up, fork over the money in the checkout line and zip back home. Unfortunately, you're not the one who usually does the grocery shopping. When you get home, your spouse takes one look at the package and blanches at the price.

Ridiculous! You shouldn't have paid more than $.98 a pound for these chicken parts! You, however, had no frame of reference and didn't know what a good price for chicken should be.

It's the same with the price/earnings ratio. Unless you have a frame of reference, you might as well not bother looking at it. Here's a quick review of the p/e ratio:

• The p/e ratio means "price per earnings per share." It's a formula: Divide the stock's price per share by the earnings per share to get the p/e ratio. Remember how important those earnings numbers are?

• The p/e ratio is meaningless without a frame of reference, something to compare it to. That's why we calculate the p/e for similar companies and compare both of them to the p/e of the stock market—represented by the Standard & Poor's 500 index. You create that percentage by dividing your stock's p/e by the market's p/e.

Here again are those steps for making the p/e ratio relevent:

1. Compare one company's p/e ratio to the p/e of the entire market, usually expressed as a percentage (i.e., ABC's p/e is 133 percent of the market's).

2. Make the same calculation with a comparable company (i.e., XYZ Cog's p/e is 124 percent of the market's).

3. Learn the trading history of the companies you're interested in so you'll know when a company's p/e ratio is relatively high or relatively low against its historical range.

4. Be aware of when one company is peaking or another is dropping.

• The p/e is a way to express how much investors are willing to pay for every dollar's worth of earnings. If your stock's p/e is 16, that could be crudely translated to say, "I'd pay $16 for every dollar in earnings my company makes."

Although the p/e ratio is a handy tool for letting investors compare one stock with another, it is only that: A single tool. You'll need a lot more than that to make an intelligent decision about what to buy and what to sell. It's the same with the chicken in the grocery store. You don't buy a package of chicken just because it is $.98 a pound. Perhaps the chicken is on sale, which obviously affects the price. Or, consider this: That price would be fantastic if we were talking about boneless chicken breasts, but not so hot if we were talking about giblets. Or maybe, truth be told, your recipe would be better served by ground chuck at $1.49 a pound.

10

Just the Facts

Remember Fruit of the Loom? Early in the book, I recounted the tale of how we bought the company with high expectations because analysts predicted good earnings—$3.20 a year per share as I recall—and we figured T-shirts were in short enough supply that the company would make a killing. We were wrong. T-shirts were in abundance because Fruit of the Loom was making more of them than they could sell. They ramped up production so much, they overdid it. Not only that, their earnings didn't come in as expected. Oops!

Meanwhile, I've been investing in long-distance telephone companies. No matter where you turn, all you hear about is the "information superhighway." Information is instant, communication is king and the superhighway has to be paved with something. Why not long-distance, fiber-optic cable? AT&T, MCI, Mexican Telephone—all these are strong companies, and they're all finding enormous growth areas overseas, where long-distance phone service has been slow to spread. Looks like an opportunity to me.

Two simple anecdotes. Two different ideas.

At the core of both is a simple word: information.

For investors, information is their food, water and air. A hearty diet of information, seasoned with a little savvy and a lot of common sense, will help make an investment portfolio grow big and strong. Don't pay attention to the information that's available or don't heed what it's saying, and your investments will be anemic.

Take Philip Morris, for example. I spent years as a major investor in the company, paying close attention to every move it made. The company grew wildly, particularly during the heyday of food companies and the takeover mania of the 1980s (when "Big Mo" first bought General Foods, then Kraft). I paid attention—a lot of attention. I watched cigarette prices increase consistently, I watched food prices on the grocery shelves, I watched smoking liability cases wend their way through the courts and into the U.S. Supreme Court. I watched as lawyers debated whether cigarette companies should take the blame (and pay big bucks in damages) for smokers who later died of cancer. In fact, I became well enough informed on the subject, I figured I could have a decent debate with just about 99 percent of the people on Wall Street.

In a sense, I was right to pay that much attention to the issue. And, in a sense, I was wrong.

I studied and kept informed, and in the final analysis I believed that the tobacco liability suits would do nothing to hurt Philip Morris (or any other cigarette maker, for that matter). Those companies might have seen sales slip in the United States, but they were selling cigarettes like gangbusters in other parts of the world. Nobody in Europe, for example, was paying any attention to Rose Cipollone and her family's case in the Supreme Court. The issue wasn't affecting the stock. I was waiting for bad news to jump down from the trees, but I was watching the wrong tree.

Instead, the price of cigarettes got killed. People started getting fed up with $2.50 a pack for their Marlboro's and started switching to off-brands. The name-brand cigarettes suffered, and Philip Morris's stock price suffered along with it. The price fell from nearly

$90 a share in September 1982 to $48 a share about a year later. I reduced my holdings in the company, but I didn't do it soon enough. I overstayed a good thing and lost some money.

I wasn't watching the right place at the right time, or worse, if I had seen what was happening with the price of cigarettes, then I wasn't paying attention. All the highly paid analysts I relied on were asleep as well. I had good, hard, tangible information in front of me, and I didn't use it wisely.

Not so with Seaboard Coastline Railroad, a below-average railroad company in the early 1970s that performed well enough and always paid a solid dividend, divvying up a share of the profits to its shareholders every year. They always had a comfortable cushion too, because they usually earned two-and-a-half times what they'd pay in their dividend. Suddenly, a news report came out that the company was cutting its dividend—serious news. Bad news. Absurd news. So absurd, in fact, that I was pretty sure it was wrong. Companies don't cut their dividend unless their earnings are down, and they don't expect to make enough money. Cut your dividends and you might as well open the window and shout, "We're in trouble!"

I started to sell some of my shares in Seaboard, slowly, waiting to see if the rumor was true. It was. Then the stock collapsed. I had about 30 minutes to sell. As it turned out, they weren't in trouble. The management, ineptly, decided it just didn't want to pay out that kind of dividend anymore. They decided, for some reason, they wanted to be a growth stock, which they weren't. Dumb.

That time, I had the hard, tangible information (that I didn't truly believe) and I acted on it. Smart.

But sometimes, the information isn't that tangible. It doesn't always come in the form of neat numbers written in columns on a corporate report. It's more "touchy-feely"—a hunch, a feeling, a perception, an idea about what you see happening in the world around you. That's what we watched in the drug companies. For example, we looked ahead to the drugs they were producing and what effect they might have on their business. Were these run-of-the-mill drugs that would slightly expand an existing market or were they blockbuster drugs that would revolutionize health care by creating a whole new market, as cholesterol drugs did? These are some of the questions you need to ask.

Speaking of a "blockbuster," that's the sort of thinking we had used to monitor the fortunes of Blockbuster Entertainment. Remember, that's the company that instantly hooked me with a good story and good management—particularly the guy who "knows every intersection in America." I liked the way Blockbuster had dominated the home video market, but the company had its share of bad news from time to time. Most of it (again) involves the coming of the information superhighway. Will there come a day when we won't even have to leave the house to get the movie of our choice beamed into our homes? That's what investors asked about Blockbuster—at least, that's what they asked when Blockbuster was publicly traded.

Before its merger with the Viacom communications empire in September 1994, the company had done a lot of diversification, buying a stake in movie companies and other entertainment avenues such as the Discovery Zone indoor playgrounds. Since that merger, Viacom has become the second largest entertainment company on earth—second only to Time Warner.

All these corporate mergings and machinations are, of course, less tangible than corporate earnings, dividends and the price of the product. But both the tangible (like Fruit of the Loom) and the intangible (like my thoughts on long-distance phone service) types of information are vital. One usually affects the other. And I don't traffic in miracles. If a story is good, I need to know why. I need a good story and a good stock price, one that is competitive with others in its industry—and preferably cheaper. I need to understand the industry. If you have a "miracle" story to tell me, you'd better be able to back it up with the right information and explain it to me in a few minutes. Otherwise, go find another investor.

The information you need is out there, available to anyone, whether you're an individual investor or an institutional investor.

Nobody (legally) plays the market with secret information, although a lot of people think they do. Just because I'm a billion-dollar player in the stock market and analysts call with every fast-breaking news story doesn't mean I have it any easier than you do—or any harder, for that matter. Although I'm watching my portfolio every minute of the day, you don't need to sweat every fast-breaking news story about a company you've bought.

If you charted the market activity of a stock hour by hour and month by month, you'd probably notice that the curves in the long-term chart would be a little smoother, but both have their ups and downs. You wouldn't notice the day-to-day things that affect a stock if you only looked month by month—and that's an advantage to individual investors. You don't have eight hours a day to watch your stocks. You don't need to.

The fact is, individuals are slowly becoming an endangered species in the stock market. Back 25 or 35 years ago, individuals made the market. Their trades were what mattered. Institutional investors were inconsequential. A book about the October 1987 crash called, appropriately enough, *Crash!*, by Avner Arbel and Albert F. Kaff, notes that in the late 1970s, individuals accounted for about 1 in 3 stock exchange transactions; that was down to 1 in 10 by 1983.

In a sense, individuals are playing on a different ballfield. The institutional investors—the folks running money for major pension plans and mutual funds—are the ones that are jumping every time an earnings estimate changes by a dime. They're the ones who read every report and act on the fast-breaking news. They create the short-term trends that buffet individual investors from day to day. Bad news hits ABC Widget, and a bunch of shares go up for sale; the price falls. But the long-term trends (Are bad times looming for widget companies?) are beyond the reach of any investor—big or small. For the secret to that future, we're all dipping into the same trough of information.

So, where is it?

As far as I'm concerned, it's not on television. There's nothing I need on TV that's going to make me a better investor. And there's almost always something else I'd rather do than watch television. For a time, about the only show I would watch was *Cheers*, and then only the daily reruns. I never watched the new shows because I never remembered to tune in on Thursday nights. Oh well. I figure I'll get to them eventually.

The second thing you don't need is reams and reams of corporate reports and analysts' tip sheets. I have stacks of them on my desk. I get them through the mail, through my fax machine (the most annoying invention in the history of the world) and through my computer. I even read some of them. But the truth is, by the time the word gets written down in a report somewhere, and by the time you get around to reading it, it's probably already taken its toll on the price of your stock—good or bad. Their value is not in what they tell you will happen to a stock in the short term. They are valuable for learning about what, in the long term, affects a company. It gives you information for your storehouse.

If I were stranded on a desert island with my portfolio, I'd need food and water to sustain me and a few other things to sustain my stocks. Of course, I'd like to have my telephone, but let's assume that's out of the question—buy and sell orders will become messages in a bottle. When the bottle comes back, I'll expect a few things inside it:

VALUE LINE

If I had a choice of only one thing to sustain me and my investments, this would be it. The *Value Line Investment Survey* includes information on at least 2,000 stocks, each company condensed into a page full of charts, graphs and text. It tells me what the company's earnings were, are and probably will be, just like you'd expect a good analyst to do. It plots a dozen different types of tangible information—numbers—the same way and it provides a few paragraphs of detail about some of those intangibles that we talked about earlier.

Look at IBM, for example.

In late 1991 and early 1992, the company finished a round of layoffs, reducing its corporate work force by 20,000. Then, Big Blue embarked on another round of cuts and a restructuring of its massive corporate profile. Instead of a giant barge floating through the world of computers, IBM was going to become a flotilla of smaller ships, each headed in the same direction, but each responsible for its own course. In a few paragraphs, *Value Line* put it another way, describing these individual ships as "independent business units" that had more freedom to make decisions about how to respond to the computer market and competitors in each of their areas.

This is the sort of "intangible" piece of information you can read and evaluate in the context of every other piece of information you gather. Is it a good idea for IBM to create "IBUs"?

That "context" fills the rest of the page, with numbers updated for the last three months, the last time *Value Line* got around to analyzing IBM. What are some of the key numbers?

Earnings per share, of course, is one: They were weak for 1991 and the publication cut its estimate for 1992 by $1.75, reducing it to $7 a share for the year. The price-earnings ratio: It was 20.4 at the time of this report (the stock price was 20.4 times higher than the company's earnings). *Value Line* even goes to the trouble of providing the relative p/e ratio—IBM's p/e ratio versus the market. IBM sold at a 25 percent premium to the market at the time; if you'd been following IBM for a while, you could judge whether that was cheap or expensive compared to the market and other computer makers. If you haven't, then take at look at the chart: The relative p/e ratio for IBM was about as high as it has ever been since 1981. And it had sold as cheaply as 77 percent of the market multiple in 1990. Maybe IBM was overpriced; I might have thought about selling it at the time.

Although *Value Line* will tell you whether you should buy the stock or sell it, the interpretation of the data and the recommendation, as always, is up to you.

By the way, it won't surprise you to know that I can point to one other advantage of *Value Line*: It's cheap. You can usually read a copy of it for free at most public libraries. If you prefer to curl up at home with it, a one-year subscription costs $525 and can be ordered on the phone at 800-833-0046.

THE WALL STREET JOURNAL

Value Line is fine for the long-term stuff, but it's not very well suited to help with the short term. The publishers only get around to each company once every three months, so the news isn't exactly hot by the time it gets into your hands. That's why you need something to keep up with the daily ebbs and flows of the market. Is Blockbuster buying anything today? How are they hedging against the coming of interactive television service with videos on demand in your living room? Why is IBM laying off all those people? What effect will the departure of General Motors' chief executive officer have on the stock price? And what about those plant closings in Michigan?

This is the kind of basic day-to-day information you need to keep track of so you know the environment your companies are operating in. I spend about four minutes a day reading *The Wall Street Journal* (*WSJ*) because the publishers are writing about things that I already heard the day before from analysts, brokers, traders and my colleagues. You don't have all those people at your disposal; you need to find that information somewhere.

Obviously, the most important part of the *WSJ* can be found in the back—the stock quotes. We said earlier they were the market's mouthpiece.

But the *WSJ* can also help you as an investor keep up with what some of those numbers mean. Frankly, an announcement about corporate earnings for the last quarter doesn't mean too much unless you know what went into it. There could be garbage in it. And the *WSJ* doesn't do a perfect job of sorting the numbers out.

Suppose, buried somewhere on page 5 of the *WSJ*, you see a small article about ABC Widget's announcing its third-quarter earnings for 1993. The report notes that ABC earned $.50 a share. You're delighted. You only expected the company to make $.40 a share. Read a few more paragraphs. "Oh," you say to yourself. "There's the punch line." ABC sold its factory in Peoria to ACME Conglomerate. The money ABC made on that sale added $.12 per share to the company's quarterly earnings. But that $.12, in my view, is not earnings, it's garbage—a balance sheet item. ABC didn't make that $.12 by selling more widgets, finding a cheaper source of raw materials or streamlining its manufacturing process. It's a one-shot boost in earnings.

ABC looked like it had a banner third-quarter, earning $.10 more than analysts expected. In fact, the company slumped and earned $.02 less than everyone expected. Now, again, it's up to you to decide what to do with that information. Maybe nothing. But at least you have the information.

AND THIS COULDN'T HURT EITHER

If the bottles that washed up onto my beach also included a few annual reports now and then, I wouldn't throw them back either. In many respects, this is the same sort of information you can get from *Value Line*. But it sure doesn't hurt to know how to read an annual report—and what the numbers mean. By the way, I'm talking about the rough, pulpy pages written by the accountants, not the glossy, colorful pages written by the public relations firms they hire. We're looking for the stuff, not the fluff.

On the next page, we can look at the 1990 annual report for ABC Widget Co., which includes financial highlights for the last five years. It can tell us a great deal about what shape this company is in. The news right off the top is pretty good. Sales have gone up every year, almost doubling in the last five years. That obviously is positive. The cost of sales—the next line down—is also important and pretty much self-explanatory. How much did it cost ABC to sell $44 million worth of widgets? It cost $17 million in raw materials, promotions, advertising and whatever else went into that cost. You don't want to see that number get too far out of line, with the cost of sales rising faster than actual sales. If your company boosts sales, but spends too much money doing it, then that doesn't help the bottom line much, does it?

Jump down a couple of lines to "Selling, General and Administrative." That's the president's salary and the cost of the central office workers. It's also the commissions for salespeople, office rent, supplies, telephone charges, advertising and recruitment costs. That item has also ballooned in recent years. That would be an area of concern, and it probably should be one of the first areas to be cut if times get tough.

Financial Highlights, ABC Widget Co., 1990 Report

	1990	1989	1988	1987	1986	1985
Statement of Income Data (In thousands, except per-share)						
Net Sales	$44,113	$39,726	$34,475	$28,765	$24,958	$24,079
Cost of Sales	17,099	16,528	15,846	13,983	12,024	10,681
Research & Develop.	7,684	5,525	5,030	4,441	5,074	5,401
Selling, General and Administrative	14,343	12,654	10,231	8,033	6,478	6,084
Income Operations	5,023	5,019	3,368	2,308	1,382	1,913
Other Income	1,778	825	314	33	24	101
Income before Taxes	6,801	5,844	3,682	2,341	1,406	2,014
Provision for Taxes	2,448	2,045	1,383	517	350	626
Income before Extra-ordinary Item	4,353	3,799	2,299	1,824	1,056	1,388
Extraordinary Item	-	—	—	—	—	401

(continued)	1990	1989	1988	1987	1986	1985
Net Income	4,353	3,799	2,299	1,824	1,056	1,789
Per Share Data Weighted Average Shares Outstanding	6,244	5,876	5,205	5,167	5,123	4,882
Earnings Per Share	$0.70	$0.65	$0.44	$0.35	$0.21	$0.37
Book Value Per Share	$5.34	$4.89	$3.45	$3.00	$2.64	$2.55
Balance Sheet Data (In thousands)						
Current Assets	$35,514	$30,685	$20,269	$19,267	$16,613	$17,614
Current Liabilities	4,532	3,350	3,409	4,227	2,848	4,682
Long-Term Debt	2,000	2,000	2,000	2,000	2,000	2,000
Total Assets	39,861	34,237	23,690	22,064	19,457	20,723
Long-term Portion of Capital Lease Obligations	—	161	311	318	1,084	1,596
Stockholders' Equity	33,329	28,726	17,970	15,519	13,524	12,444
Current Ratio	7.8 to 1	9.2 to 1	5.9 to 1	4.6 to 1	5.8 to 1	3.8 to 1
Other Data						
Number of Employees	296	251	230	240	218	239
Sales Per Average # of Employees	$161	$165	$147	$126	$109	$128

Otherwise, if things seem to be going fine, this is probably okay. You don't want to see this number increase as a percentage of revenues too much. But you don't want to cut management unless it's doing a lousy job.

In the per-share data, it's not surprising to see the number of outstanding shares grow a little every year, particularly in a growth company (which we will assume ABC is). Nor is it a surprise to see earnings per share increasing every year. Remember: They'd better. Otherwise, we have a problem with ABC, right? The key, of course, is whether ABC has met analysts' expectations for earnings. That can't be determined here. Book value per share is a theoretical value of the company if it were liquidated and given to its shareholders—in a word, it's total assets ($39,861,000) minus liabilities ($6,532,000) divided by outstanding shares (6,244). Some investors look for takeover targets by buying stocks that are selling for less than book value. (Book value is much more important for financial companies than for industrial ones. For financial companies, their assets are easily converted into dollars because that's all they really have. For industrial companies, it is much more difficult to determine the tangible value of a patent or a trademark, which might be included in the company's theoretical book value.)

The current ratio is a good number to watch too. Dividing current assets by current liabilities, it shows how capable the company is to handle stormy economic weather in the coming year. The lower the ratio, the worse off the company. It's the same with the company's debt ratio. ABC doesn't break that out for us in this chart; we have to figure it out ourselves. Figure that ratio by dividing long-term debt by the shareholder's equity plus long-term debt. For ABC, long-term debt is $2,000. Divide by $35,329 (long-term debt plus shareholder's equity). That comes to a ratio of 5.7 percent. And that is very low.

One more: Sales per employee. A simple number, but one that you'd like to see go up, if possible. Until 1990, ABC's workers were becoming more and more productive every year. Inflation itself should make these numbers go up.

These are simple sources of information, but they are critical. They are also supplementary to whatever you can wring out of your stockbroker, who is supposed to be doing something to earn that commission. If you have questions about your stocks, call and ask— assuming you're not stranded on that desert island. That's the broker's job.

I said earlier that nobody expects individual investors to spend eight hours a day poring over stocks tables and analysts' reports. It's not possible and it's not necessary. But if you're interested in investing money in the the stock market, you've got to spend time paying attention to the stocks you're buying. There's no such thing as a get-rich-quick scheme, and there's no such thing as gain without pain. If you're not willing to watch and act and adjust—if you're not comfortable owning stocks—don't bother. Buy a mutual fund and let someone else do it for you.

11

Paper Money

I started investing exactly the wrong way. I bought one stock, 10 shares worth of it, and I watched as economic and political forces pumped it up and battered it down, until finally, I managed to eke a small profit out of it—without knowing the reason at all. I did not diversify, I did not pay attention to the reasons I bought, I did not know why I should sell. In short, I basically broke every piece of advice I've passed along in this book. Every piece but one: At least I *started*. And I started early.

That's more than I can say for a lot of people who haven't even tried to invest their money wisely in the stock market.

In truth, I might have had a better start than some novices. I really started investing because I saw my grandfather do it with some small measure of success. I had a small part in helping him by reading stock quotes out of the paper and listening to his discussions during the periodic visits with his broker. Any little thing you can do to start erasing the mystery and confusion of the stock market makes it that much easier to start participating in it. Too many "experts" relish the idea of making the market as confusing and baffling as can be. It makes them look all the more important; after all, they are the ones who can navigate these shark-infested waters. If anything, this book should persuade you that the stock market isn't just for "experts" in the big city. It's for people who want to make money, wherever they are.

For me, it's nice when even the experts can be tripped up. Like every profession, investors use a lot of phrases and buzzwords to make their language sound foreign to outsiders. I recall a few years ago talking to a financial head from a large corporation in a meeting with the president of my bank. I started talking about RBOCs. He thought I was discussing gym shoes when I was actually using the acronym for Regional Bell Operating Companies, the seven smaller Bells that resulted from the breakup of AT&T.

Still, there's even more you can do to make yourself familiar with the stock market and the companies that are traded every day. In Florida, public and private schoolchildren follow this piece of advice every day in a game run by the University of Central Florida. It is called, simply enough, The Stock Market Game.

These students form investment clubs in their school math class or social studies class, three or four students to a club, hundreds of clubs around the state. Each club gets $250,000 in capital to invest as they choose during a 10-week term. And it doesn't break the state's education budget. The money is only make-believe, and their portfolio is only on paper. That was my advice a few chapters ago: Minimize the cost of on-the-job training. Start a paper portfolio of stocks and track their stories, their prices and their p/e ratios so you know how the market moves—and how it moves your stocks.

Thousands of Florida students (and students in other states too, probably) do it successfully year after year. Some have reaped whopping returns in 10 weeks. Of course, anyone who truly invests with only a 10-week horizon is a fool. And, of course, teachers aren't doing it to make Wall Street investment barons out of the student body. They expect the students to learn a little math, some economics, a bit of social studies and do a lot of reading during the course of the game. It doesn't hurt, of course, that they learn how the market works, how to read a stock page or an analyst's report or how to do research on a company. It may come in handy years later, when they have some *real* money to invest.

You can do the same thing. Find 10, 20, 30, 40 or 50 stocks you like. Have a good reason for liking them and write it down along with the stocks and the price you paid. Track those prices and those companies for a few weeks and decide whether the reasons you liked them are still there. This exercise has a few advantages.

First, you can develop a style that suits you. I'm not good at investing in commodities, so I don't. I stick to the things I know and leave the rest to people I trust. I typically don't buy foreign stocks, for example. I don't expect someone from another country to invest in American companies better than I can; why should I expect to outperform someone from another country on his or her home turf? With a paper portfolio you can determine what stocks you seem to have a knack for following and understanding, assuming you apply yourself with the same gusto you'd use with real money.

Second, a paper portfolio starts to give you some background on the companies you will want to track. Jumping headfirst into the stock market without any background is like betting on the horses without reading the *Daily Racing Form.* You can bet on a horse by plunking down your cash on any horse with a clever name, or you can figure out which ones tend to do better on a muddy track. It's the same with the stock market. If you're frightened away from a stock because the price is $100 a share, you're missing the point. You must know where that stock historically has traded and the range of its price/earnings ratio. You need to be able to compare that with the p/e of other similar companies and to the stock market as a whole before you know whether $100 is a bargain or a rip-off. You can get that history and that experience almost as well with fake money as with real money.

That, of course, is the third advantage. None of this experience costs you a dime. This is the safest investment portfolio you'll ever see. You can set up a portfolio as large as you want, with as much money as you want, because it's all fake. Of course, you won't make any money either until you put some cold cash behind the experience you're collecting.

So what does a paper portfolio look like?

Below, you'll see mine. I assembled it based on stock prices on December 31, 1992, for companies that are representative of the kinds of companies I was buying at the time. I promise: I didn't pick these stocks because I knew how they'd do in the future. That will be apparent as we examine a few blunders I made in this particular portfolio.

Let's take a look.

Tony's Paper Portfolio from Dec. 31, 1992

Stock	Shares	Price	Assets	%
AUTOS				
Chrysler	500	32.000	$16,000	1.6%
General Motors	900	32.250	29,025	2.9
Goodyear	300	68.375	20,513	2.1
CONSUMER STAPLES				
Philip Morris	400	77.125	30,850	3.1
Coca-Cola	600	41.875	25,125	2.5
Cott Corp.	1000	25.250	25,250	2.5
Procter & Gamble	600	53.625	32,175	3.2
CYCLICALS				
Conrail	400	47.500	19,000	1.9
Whirlpool	400	44.625	17,850	1.8
Minnesota Mining	200	100.625	20,125	2.0

(continued)

Stock	Shares	Price	Assets	%
ELECTRICAL				
General Electric	600	85.500	51,300	5.1
ENERGY				
Texaco	400	59.750	23,900	2.4
Unocal	800	25.500	20,400	2.0
BANKS/OTHER FINANCIAL				
Bankamerica	600	46.500	27,900	2.8
Chemical Bank	600	38.625	23,175	2.3
First Union	600	43.625	26,175	2.6
Marsh McLennan	200	91.375	18,275	1.8
Unum	400	53.000	21,200	2.1
Merrill Lynch	300	59.500	17,850	1.8
HEALTH				
Glaxo	1000	23.750	23,750	2.4
Johnson & Johnson	600	50.500	30,300	3.0
Merck	700	43.375	30,363	3.0
U.S. Healthcare	700	44.625	31,328	3.1
LEISURE				
Blockbuster	1000	18.750	18,750	1.9
Mattel	800	25.375	20,300	2.0
McDonald's	600	48.750	29,250	2.9

(continued)

Stock	Shares	Price	Assets	%
MEDIA				
CBS	200	188.000	37,600	3.8
Gannett	600	50.750	30,450	3.0
RETAIL				
Costco	800	24.500	19,600	2.0
Dayton Hudson	200	75.750	15,150	1.5
Federated Dept. Store	1000	19.750	19.750	2.0
Fruit of the Loom	400	48.625	19,450	1.9
Toys "R" Us	500	40.125	20,063	2.0
Wal-Mart	800	32.000	25,600	2.6
TECHNOLOGY				
EDS (General Motors E)	600	32.875	19,725	2.0
Novell	600	28.500	17,100	1.7
Pitney Bowes	600	39.875	23,925	2.4
Storage Technology	800	20.250	16,200	1.6
TELEPHONE				
AT&T	700	51.000	35,700	3.6
Telephonos de Mexico	600	56.000	33,600	3.4
CASH			16,050	1.6%
TOTAL ASSETS			$1,000,000	100.0%

Highlights of the Portfolio

As you can see, I wasn't bashful about running a portfolio with make-believe money. I started out with a million bucks. Why not? What's to stop you from starting with that much? The idea is the same whether you start with a million or $10,000. I bought between 200 and 1,000 shares of every stock in my portfolio; you don't have to buy that much—or you could buy more. I bought stock in 40 different companies representing 13 different industries. That is a fairly well diversified portfolio, easily large enough to give an individual investor a cushion against calamity in one industry or another. But maybe you're not comfortable keeping track of that many stocks. That's fine too. As I said, this is an exercise to determine what you are comfortable doing and how you're comfortable doing it.

You may recall earlier in the book that I talked about General Motors. Well, this portfolio opens up at about the time GM started to look good to me, so I included it with my stock picks—900 shares worth $29,025. But even with that exposure, GM took less than 3 percent of my portfolio. Why include it?

In my view, the 1980s were the Ford years, when the company introduced new cars and new styles and basically made big strides with American car buyers. It seemed like time for another car company to have a chance, and General Motors seemed to have a few things going for it. The company's chief executive officer was in trouble at the time (he wasn't gone yet), but they were introducing new models, and they were starting to cut costs and talk about closing plants—something GM desperately needed to do. Meanwhile, Chrysler also looked pretty good, mostly because of its new product line and improving profitablity. I bought that too.

Another point of interest in this portfolio: The banking industry. We'll talk more later about why I liked it. In a word, it was changing. It was an industry that seemed due for good things as banks expanded into services such as mutual funds and other investment opportunities. Their bad loans were decreasing rapidly. Also, big banks were buying out smaller ones, and that's always a good time to buy into an industry, particularly if you can find the banks that are takeover targets. That almost certainly means a profit, both before the takeover, when rumors start driving up the stock price and during the takeover, when the buyer needs to pay a premium for shareholders' stock.

In all cases, the companies you see included in the original portfolio are there because they are part of an industry I like or feel that I must pay attention to. More important, those companies are there because I believe they are good, sound companies with solid balance sheets and reasonable growth potential—they also happened to look cheap at the time, relative to the market and other stocks in their industry. This valuation is important. Refer to Chapter 9 ("What's It Worth to You?") on valuing stocks and the p/e ratio.

The industry that commands the largest share of this portfolio is one of my favorites, one that was also a good performer during the 1980s, when consumers were spending money as fast—and usually faster—than they could get it. Retailers were in their heyday during the 1980s, and at the end of 1992, I still hadn't soured on the industry. In my paper portfolio, retailers make up 12 percent of my investments. Besides the reasons I just mentioned for picking stocks, there's another good reason I am fond of the retailing industry. You'll be surprised at the simplicity of it.

Frankly, I just understand it better than any other industry. Buy what you know. If you don't invest in something you know, you can't know when to sell because you won't understand what affects the stocks. I know retailing. Everybody who has ever gone into a store knows retailing.

Health care stocks were also a strong holding for me during the 1980s, and as you'll see later in the book, they were something I held for too long. That is reflected in this portfolio as well; health and drug stocks represent the second-largest share of the total, 11.5 percent.

And after all my badmouthing about how much I hate computers and high technology, you'll notice that I have a fairly sizable position—7.7 percent—in technology stocks. This also reflects what was happening in my "real" portfolio at the time. In early 1991, we barely owned any technology stocks, which suited me just fine. Then, for a variety of reasons, it looked like the time for technology to get a good ride. It had done poorly for a decade (although some companies had flourished). With the improving economy, it seemed like the right time for companies that sell consumer electronics and parts for personal computers; for corporate America, it seemed like the right time to expect them to improve productivity, which often means improving their own computer systems.

That put me on the horns of a dilemma: I thought technology ought to work, but I hate technology. So I decided not to bet the farm on it and to buy a few different companies that look good. And avoid personal computer companies like lightning on the golf course—they're too volatile, the price of computers is falling, they have too much product on the market. If I hate technology, you can bet I *detest* personal computer companies. In my real portfolio, technology rose from about 3 percent to 9 percent of my holdings, and it worked pretty well for me. That doesn't mean I suddenly loved technology.

Let's put it another way: I have *always* said I don't like the airline industry, but there are times when I will say it's a good place to invest for the short term. It can be the same with technology.

Trading Is Where the Money Is Made

Now we can spend a little time discussing the trades I made in my paper portfolio through 1993. These, of course, were made before Federated Department Stores and Macy's merged in November 1994; before Blockbuster, Viacom and Paramount became an entertainment colossus in the same year; before I knew anything about the stacks of T-shirts piling up in Fruit of the Loom warehouses. All those news events obviously complicate the investment landscape for those particular companies. But that's what makes investing fun. What does it *mean*? And how can I capitalize?

I'll show you all the trades I made throughout the 12 months we're going to look at, but we'll only discuss some of the highlights and reasons behind the trades. At the end of each month, I looked at the entire portfolio and decided which companies should go, which should stay and which should join the group. You'll see the results, and you'll notice that I did a few things that I don't usually do. For example, in my professional investments, I've said before that I turn over 100 percent of my stock in a year's time. Beyond that, I am a very active stock trader in the office. I can buy and sell a company in the same day if it seems as though the price has gone from cheap to expensive that quickly.

In this case, I did neither.

I made 32 trades in a year's time. I sold stock in 16 companies that I owned at the start of the year and purchased stock in 15 companies—one of them twice. I only bought or sold at the end of each month. And that, my friends, is something any careful investor ought to be able to manage between keeping up with a job, a house and a family.

Let's take a look at some of my trades.

Date	*B/S*	*Share*	*Company*	*Price*	*Reason*	*Net$*	*Gain*
2-28-93	Sell	800	Costco	20.000	Poor sales	16,000	(3,600)
3-30-93	Sell	200	Dayton Hudson	71.250	Poor California sales	14,250	(200)
	Buy	900	Magna Int'l	33.500	Looked like good auto supplier		(30,150)
4-30-93	Sell	200	Minn. Mining	111.250	Price too high	22,250	2,125
	Sell	800	Unocal	30.625	Price too high	24,500	4,100
	Buy	300	Royal Dutch	88.750	Stock price looks cheap		(26,625)
	Sell	600	Bankamerica	46.250	Calif. economy is doing poorly	27,750	(150)

(continued)

Date	B/S	Share	Company	Price	Reason	Net$	Gain
	Buy	500	Chemical Bank	38.250	Cheap stock price		(19,125)
	Sell	400	Fruit of the Loom	40.750	High inventory	16,300	(3,150)
	Sell	700	Merck	37.000	Earnings per share declining; so was growth	25,900	(4,463)
	Sell	1000	Glaxo	18.375	EPS declining	18,375	(5,375)

We've completed four months of the year. If I were a squeamish investor, I might look at these results and start running for the phone book, dialing every bank in my neighborhood looking for the best rate on a certificate of deposit. Fortunately, I'm not a squeamish investor, and you shouldn't be either. If you're not able to ride out a few bad times, then maybe it's true; maybe the stock market isn't for you. We all take our lumps from time to time. Clearly, I took a few lumps here.

Out of the eight stocks that I sold, I lost money on six of them.

Remember the keys to picking and holding a company: If you're confident that several companies in an industry are good and solid with strong fundamentals, then select the one that is cheaper, based on p/e ratios and where the market is; but if the fundamentals change, then you don't want to be associated with those companies. It becomes difficult to judge their value. That's what happened to several stocks on the list so far. Take Costco, for example, poor sales were hurting its bottom line. Later in the year, Costco merged with Price Club. Dayton-Hudson fared no better. With Fruit of the Loom, we've discussed their inventory problems already. But were there problems the company was trying to hide by banking an enormous inventory? Did they think they could fool investors into thinking they wouldn't have to cut prices on T-shirts or slow down their manufacturing? Don't be silly; of course not.

Bankamerica is heavily linked to the California economy; as the state goes, so goes the company. At the same time, Chemical Bank's price looked cheap compared with Bankamerica's.

Part of your job as an investor is to identify the doggie stocks and banish them to the pound. When a company and its stock isn't performing, I get rid of it and move on. There's no time to waste hoping it will recover or berating yourself for losing money. That's time you could spend finding the success stories in the market. And we did find some success stories in this first lot—two of them.

Unocal is a holding company for the Union Oil Company of California, which produces oil and natural gas and operates gas stations in seven states. For my purposes, the company was solid, and I simply did what comes naturally: Buy cheap. When Unocal's price got ahead of itself, that's when I sold. And that's what I meant in the just-mentioned trading chart when I said, "Price too high."

The same goes for Minnesota Mining and Manufacturing, a boring name for a company that is anything but boring. You might know the company better by its more popular name: 3M. And if you've ever wrapped a Christmas present, sanded down a rough tabletop, videotaped a television program or jotted a message on a sticky piece of note paper, chances are you've crossed paths with 3M. The company manufactures an estimated 60,000 products, including Scotch tape, sandpaper, videotape and Post-It message pads. This enormous company—nearly $14 billion in sales worldwide in 1992—started in 1902 when five businessmen started selling corundum—an abrasive mineral—to manufacturers of grinding wheels. In 1916, the company paid its first dividend to stockholders and has never missed a quarterly dividend payment since. The company, despite its size, had streamlined a bit in the past few years by reducing labor costs per product by 35 percent. In a word, 3M is a good company.

The only question, then, is whether the $100.63 a share price was reasonable when I bought it. Obviously, I thought it was a bargain. The novice investor looks at the price—$100 *for every share*—and gets scared off. The wise investor knows $100 is meaningless without context. What are you buying? The answer here is a good company at a reasonable price, selling at the low end of the range where investors have traded it in the past. The purchase price was near the bottom of 3M's p/e range of 17 times earnings. When the price hit $111.25 a share and the high end of its range (19 times earnings), that's when 3M started to look a little expensive. Time to sell.

It was a good idea too. By the end of the year, the price had slid back down more than two points to $108.75. The market was catching up with what I already knew: 3M was overpriced at $111. I was also right about Unocal. By the end of the year, the company's stock price had dropped $2.75.

My purchases in the first four months of the year included Magna International, an auto parts supplier. If I think automakers are going to do okay, then I figured the companies supplying parts to those manufacturers ought to do pretty well too. Again, I was right this time. Magna's stock price rose 10 points in eight months.

I also bought into Royal Dutch, another enormous company, which, combined with the Shell Group, forms the world's largest petroleum and natural gas company. Again, it was a case of a company's looking cheap in an industry I liked. We'll see how it does.

Now, let's check back in with our portfolio and see about a few more trades during the second quarter of the year.

Date	B/S	Share	Company	Price	Reason	Net$	Gain
5-31-93	Sell	600	Johnson & John.	44.625	Health/ drug industry was collapsing	26,775	(3,525)
	Buy	1400	Medco	28.750	Growing 30%/yr.	(40,250)	
	Buy	300	McDonald's	49.750	EPS accelerating	(14,925)	
	Sell	500	Toys "R" Us	39.250	Sales slipping	19,625	(438)
6-30-93	Buy	800	Imperial Chemical	39.625	Restructuring		(31,700)

(continued)

Date	B/S	Share	Company	Price	Reason	Net$	Gain
	Buy	1400	China Fund	16.875	I love China		(23,625)
	Sell	600	First Union	48.500	Reducing banks	29,100	2,925
	Buy	300	Gannett	49.750	Looks cheap		(14,925)

At the end of the first four months, you'll notice that I dumped some of my favorite stocks—health care and pharmaceuticals. Sorry, Merck; sorry, Glaxo. Both are drug companies. Both were gone. The industry was deteriorating. Growth rates and earnings estimates were coming down. We'll talk more about my *real* experiences with health stock investments, which were very successful for a long time. But for now, their appeal is eluding me. Their fortunes were ending, and I didn't want to be around for the rest of the fall. So the trend continues in this batch of trades. Good-bye to Johnson & Johnson, which is suffering right along with the rest of the bunch.

However, we can say hello to a related cousin: Medco Containment Corp.

Medco is the nation's largest mail-order pharmacy. It serves more than 29 million customers who work for some of the nation's top Fortune 500 companies, processing more than 2 million prescriptions a month. The company doesn't make drugs; it simply delivers them from the drug companies to you. I added it to my paper portfolio because its fortunes were rising at 30 percent a year. That's the kind of growth I can't afford to ignore. Lucky I added it when I did.

Less than two months later, Merck bought Medco—a merger that could do almost nothing but increase the value of my investment. By the end of the year, the value of my Medco stock price had changed from 1,400 shares of Medco at $28.75 to 1,301 shares of Merck at $34.38. I also ended with some cash in the deal, giving me a total of a 19 percent increase in six months.

Two other highlights:

- I already owned 600 shares of McDonald's, one of the 30 companies listed in the Dow Jones Industrial Average. But the price still looked good, and the company's earnings were better than expected. This was a company that had suddenly created *more* reasons to like it. So I did, to the tune of 300 more shares.

- I like China. I think China could be a great market for business as that nation's huge economy grows and becomes more industrialized. But I know zero about Chinese companies. That's why I bought 1,400 shares in a mutual fund that trades in Chinese companies or companies that do business in China. I won't go into it too much here; we'll talk more about mutual funds later in the book.

Here are the rest of the trades I made in my "paper portfolio" for the year:

Date	B/S	Share	Company	Price	Reason	Net$	Gain
8-30-93	Sell	600	EDS	31.875	Slowing growth	19,125	(600)
	Buy	600	United Health	59.250	Best HMO in the industry		(35,550)
9-30-93	Buy	300	Procter & Gamble	47.500	Growth better		(14,250)
	Sell	200	Marsh McLennan	87.250	Earnings per share are too high	17,450	(825)
	Sell	300	Merrill Lynch	98.000	Made all I want	29,400	11,550
	Sell	1000	Block-buster	28.625	Up 53 percent; made all I want	28,625	9,875

(continued)

Date	B/S	Share	Company	Price	Reason	Net$	Gain
	Buy	600	The Home Depot	38.500	Off 25 percent; lost all I want		(23,100)
	Buy	600	Wal-Mart	24.625	Off 28 percent		(14,775)
	Sell	800	Mattel	27.625	Worried about Christmas season	22,100	1,800
	Buy	800	Novell	18.875	Off 46 percent		(15,100)
	Buy	200	General Electric	95.875	Stock looks cheap now		(19,175)
10-30-93	Buy	700	MCI Comm.	28.500	Good growth		(19,950)
11-30-93	Buy	500	MCI Comm.	24.375	Awfully cheap		(12,188)

This completes the trades I made in a year's time. Let's just say I took the month of December off for Christmas and let all my investments ride for the month. In the final summary of my paper portfolio, I'll price everything out with 1993 closing prices to see how everything did. But what are the highlights from this lot of trades?

Good-bye to EDS. As I mentioned, technology stocks are often a losing proposition for me, and EDS is the kind of technology stock I usually try pretty hard to like. Election dabbler and presidential critic Ross Perot founded the company in 1962 after he left IBM. Big Blue didn't like his idea: Create a service that does all the data management and computer processing for clients, rather than forcing them to buy the hardware and hire the expertise to manage the information themselves. Perot left, built his idea into a corporate empire called Electronic Data Systems and sold it to General

Motors 22 years later for $2.5 billion. The company is still independently traded as General Motors Class "E" stock.

So I tried to like EDS for my paper portfolio. But it just sat there, doing nothing for nine months. Finally, earnings estimates started suggesting that the company's growth was slowing. Perhaps there were other places to put my money.

Take Novell, for example. Although not exactly like EDS, the company is similar in one respect: It doesn't build computers. Instead, it helps other companies figure out how to build computer networks. Again, this is more like the kind of technology stock I can handle. (According to *Hoover's Handbook of American Business*, the chief executive of this high-tech firm drives a pickup truck to work. What's not to like?) I bought 600 shares at the start of this exercise and still liked the company 10 months later, although near-term earnings were disappointing. I still liked the 1994–95 outlook. So when the price of the stock had fallen 46 percent, I decided to pull out my bushel basket again and start scooping up more Novell—another 800 shares.

The same was true with Wal-Mart and The Home Depot. The companies were strong, the stories were good, the prices were just down and the growth rates were under attack. I felt it was a buying opportunity.

At the opposite end of the scale, there's something to be said for knowing when it's time to sell. In the case of Blockbuster and Merrill Lynch, the numbers were wonderful. It was not the time to be greedy. Blockbuster had boomed by 53 percent from the time I bought it. That's plenty, particularly when I felt the stock was somewhat ahead of itself at the time. It's p/e was hovering around 28 times earnings above its typical high of 24. Meanwhile, where Merrill Lynch was concerned, I was satisfied with a stock that had gone up 65 percent in nine months—particularly in the financial industry, which I was beginning to sour on somewhat.

General Electric is also an interesting case in this portfolio exercise. It shows just how the definition of *cheap* can change. At the start of the exercise, I owned 600 shares of GE, purchased at $85.50 a share. Nine months later, I bought another 200 shares of the stock because, as I noted earlier, it was "cheap." Fact is, GE's stock was selling at $95.86 a share when I bought the 200 shares—more than $10 more than it was when we started! How can that be considered cheap?

Again, we have to remember that the price of a stock only has meaning when compared to the market and the company's range. In September 1993, when I decided to buy more GE for my paper portfolio, the stock was priced higher than it was at the start of the year, but its p/e ratio was *still* 92 percent of the Standard & Poor's 500 p/e ratio. Cheap. Extremely well run. Growing. A good company. A good buy.

Now the entire exercise is done. What are we left with?

Well, by my calculations, I lost a lot of money on some of the stocks I sold. Of the 16 stocks I sold, 10 were doggie stocks. Their combined value was $23,026 less than it was when I bought them. At the same time, 6 of the stocks I sold were ahead when I sold them, ahead by a combined total of $32,375. On balance, I made $9,349 on my trades.

I also kept a bunch of companies. Some, such as Chrysler, grew 66 percent while they were in my portfolio. Others, such as Goodyear, grew 33.8 percent in exactly the same amount of time.

But all in all, the "gainers outnumbered losers" as the newscasters sometimes say in their nightly report on Wall Street. My portfolio started out with a value of $1 million. It ended with an asset value of $1,189,134—an 18.9 percent increase in one year. That certainly beats the passbook savings account rate, doesn't it?

More important: We got interested and involved in investing.

Tony's Paper Portfolio on Dec. 31, 1993

Stock	Shares 12-31-93	Price 12-31-93	Assets 12-31-93	1 Year Gain
AUTOS				
Chrysler	500	53.250	26,625	66.4
General Motors	900	54.875	49,388	70.2

(continued)

Stock	Shares 12-31-93	Price 12-31-93	Assets 12-31-93	1 Year Gain
Goodyear	600	45.750	27,450	33.8+
Magna International	900	49.750	44,775	48.5*
CONSUMER STAPLES				
Philip Morris	400	55.625	22,250	(27.9)
Coca-Cola	600	44.625	26,775	6.6
Cott Beverage	1000	24.375	24,375	(3.5)
Procter & Gamble	900	57.000	51,300	10.5*
CYCLICALS				
Conrail	400	66.875	26,750	40.8
Whirlpool	400	66.500	26,600	49.0
Minnesota Mining	0	108.750	0	10.6@
Imperial Chemical	800	47.250	37,800	19.2*
ELECTRICAL				
General Electric	800	104.875	83,900	63.5
ENERGY				
Texaco	400	64.750	25,900	8.4
Unocal	0	27.875	0	9.3
Royal Dutch	300	104.375	31,313	17.6*
BANKS OR OTHER FINANCIAL				
Bankamerica	0	46.375	0	(0.5)@
Chemical Bank	1100	40.125	44,138	90.5

(continued)

Stock	Shares 12-31-93	Price 12-31-93	Assets 12-31-93	1 Year Gain
First Union	0	41.250	0	11.2@
Marsh McLennan	0	81.250	0	(4.5)@
Unum	400	52.500	21,000	(1.0)
Merrill Lynch	0	42.000	0	64.7@
HEALTH				
Glaxo	0	20.875	0	(22.6)@
Johnson & Johnson	0	44.875	0	(11.6)@
Merck	0	34.375	0	(14.7)@
U.S. Healthcare	700	57.625	40,338	29.1
United Healthcare	600	75.875	45,525	28.1*
Medco (MRK merger)	1301	34.375	44,722	19.6
LEISURE				
Blockbuster	0	30.625	0	52.7@
Mattel	0	27.625	0	8.9@
McDonald's	900	57.000	51,300	75.4
MEDIA				
CBS	200	288.500	57,700	53.5
Gannett	900	57.250	51,525	69.2
RETAIL				
Costco	0	NA	0	(18.4)@
Dayton Hudson	0	66.625	0	(5.9)@

(continued)

Stock	Shares 12-31-93	Price 12-31-93	Assets 12-31-93	1 Year Gain
Federated	1000	20.750	20,750	5.1
Fruit of the Loom	0	24.125	0	(16.2)@
Toys "R" Us	0	40.875	0	(2.2)@
Wal-Mart	1400	25.000	35,000	(28.1)
The Home Depot	600	39.500	23,700	2.6*
TECHNOLOGY				
EDS	0	29.250	0	(3.0)@
Novell	1400	20.750	29,050	69.9
Pitney Bowes	600	41.375	24,825	3.8
Storage Technology	800	31.875	25,500	57.4
TELEPHONE				
AT&T	700	52.500	36,750	2.9
Telephonos de Mexico	600	67.500	40,500	20.5
MCI Comm.	1200	28.250	33,900	6.9*
MISC.				
China Fund	1400	28.250	39,550	67.4*
CASH		18,163		
TOTAL ASSETS		$1,189,134	18.91%	

@ % change at time of sale during the year.

* % change since time of purchase during the year.

+ Goodyear had a 2 for 1 stock split in May.

INSIDE LINE

If you think this portfolio is typical of my real investments, think again. It's not. In this case, of the 48 companies I held at the end of the exercise, 34 of them were moneymakers. But remember what I've told you a hundred times already: If you're right 55 percent of the time, then you're ahead of the game by a long shot.

It is obvious to most people that they should not expect every stock to make a killing, ringing up gains of 30 percent or 40 percent every time you turn around. But I'll go a step further: Don't even expect every stock you buy to make money. Many won't. Look at my paper portfolio: Wal-Mart, typically one of the darlings of my investments, lost 28 percent; so did Philip Morris, another stock I usually love.

Meanwhile, a stock I like, but I'm always wary of, is General Motors. Obviously, I was right on that one and caught it at the best time: Its value climbed 70 percent in one year. It doesn't take too many like that to offset a few Wal-Marts, right?

12

Crash!

When some people come home after a bad day at work, they kick the dog, yell at their kids or drown their sorrows at a local saloon. Some hide in the pages of a good book. I prune my hedges. That's exactly what I did at about 5:30 P.M. on October 19, 1987. It was a very bad day.

I have never been the sort of person who stays late at the office when it isn't necessary. Work can wait for another workday as far as I'm concerned, and that day was no exception. Once the market had mercifully closed on that day, the day of the largest stock market decline in history, I went home, changed from suit and tie to garden clothes and pruned the hell out of those hedges. I'm amazed they survived. The pension funds I managed lost about one-quarter of their value that day. The stock market had declined 508 points, losing a record 23 percent of its value—about $600 billion.

And it wasn't exactly a surprise.

Everybody predicted a bad Monday, the day of the Crash of '87, after the terrible Friday that had preceded it, October 16. I was in Miami for a speech the previous week, and I pretended that I had not yet seen what the market had done the day before. I opened my speech with my standard question: "How'd the market do yesterday?" Everyone in the audience just laughed. It had fallen 108 points, foreshadowing a lousy week on Wall Street.

By the time we got to work the next Monday morning, sell orders had piled up. It was as if U.S. securities suddenly had contracted some dreaded social disease. Foreign investors from stock markets around the globe had put in orders to sell their U.S. stocks that day. Everyone was sure it was going to be a bad day; everyone could feel it. Nobody was talking about it. Imagine the feeling of dread you might have in the hours before a hurricane hits.

Was there panic? You can be sure of it. Was that day exciting? You better believe it. It was a seat-of-the-pants trading day like none I've ever experienced. Was it fun? Certainly not. No matter what happened, I still lost $600 million in one day. I would never describe that as "fun."

But my reports for the end of the year, December 31, 1987, were not bad at all—considering what had happened two months earlier. I beat the market. My fund was up 16 percent for the year. I did it because I had a sound investment philosophy, and I stuck with it when things looked about as bad as they could get. That philosophy has it roots in the p/e ratios we discussed in chapter 9. It's the idea that stocks can be compared with one another, played one against the other, traded one for the other. I call it "pairs trading" and it was basically all I had to work with on October 19–20, 1987.

A Little More about Pairs Trading

As you've seen in Chapter 9, I don't just buy stock in one company and while away the days until it starts to drop. I can't do business that way; I need to know how that company's competition is doing too. And I want to know whether I ought to have my money there as well.

If the economic climate is good for widget companies, it stands to reason that all the widget companies should be doing well. If they all have perfect management, perfect inventory control, perfect return on investment, perfect quality merchandise and perfect marketing, they'll all be great investments. Of course, you can guess how often that happens. The trick is finding the ones that are doing the best and riding their fortunes. That's why pairs trading is so much a part of my technique.

I put my money into Toys "R" Us while it does well and when it appears to be at the top of its game—and perhaps destined for a fall—I'll sell some Toys and switch to another retailer—perhaps The Home Depot or Wal-Mart. Or maybe all three of them! (It doesn't just have to be *pairs* trading.) I'll do the same thing with food companies like Quaker Oats and Kellogg's or with drug companies like Merck and Bristol-Myers or with publishing companies like Gannett and Tribune. Here's an example taken from my recommendation books:

September 22, 1989: We are recommending swapping Liz Claiborne (LIZC) into The Limited (LTD). These are both very good companies that we expect to do well in 1989 and 1990. The primary reason for the swap is one of price. LIZC (at $26.50 a share) is within 10 percent of where we think it can go and LTD (at $37.62) still has potential upside of 23 percent. We believe LIZC should sell between 80 percent and 105 percent of the market (remember your p/e ratios!) and LTD should sell between 110 percent and 140 percent. LIZC is near the top of the range and LTD is near the bottom.

June 27, 1990: Both LTD ($23.25) and LIZC ($32) have substantially outperformed the market in 1990, and both are selling near their highs for the year. Meanwhile, surveys of consumer sentiment are less positive than earlier, the earnings rate appears to be going up and the economy appears to be slowing. We believe that LTD and LIZC can sell at 100 percent to 130 percent and 75 percent to 95 percent of the market, respectively. Both are at the high end of their range. We would sell both.

November 19, 1990: The Gap (GPS) and LTD have traveled separate paths this year. GPS is having a record year and surpassing all expectations. LTD, on the other hand, while having a record year, is not meeting either investors' expectations or their own. Looked at another way, though, LTD is doing very well under pretty bad conditions. We believe that a switch is in order between GPS and LTD. LTD is selling at the bottom of its range (90 percent of the market) and GPS is at the top of theirs (112 percent). Yet there isn't that much different between the two. Both will grow at about 15 percent to 20 percent, have good managements, and are among the best at what they do. Thus a 22 percent difference in their p/es seems excessive. We recommend a swap.

January 7, 1991: During December The Gap's comparable store sales were up 12 percent and total sales were up 24 percent. This was stronger than any other apparel specialty chain we know. We are reinstating our buy on GPS. The switch with LTD has worked out very well with LTD up 30 percent and GPS up 9 percent. This has closed the value difference between them. We are now buyers of both stocks.

January 17, 1991: We put GPS back on the buy list 10 days ago at $33.50. It has gone up 22.4 percent and the market is up 3.3 percent. We think that GPS is ahead of itself. Take the money and run. In a market like this, we would switch the money into (retailer) Dayton Hudson, which is at $59.00. We think that in 12 to 15 months DH will be a $90.00 stock.

February 7, 1991: We put a sell on The Gap on January 17 at $41.00 and market at 371. Today the market is at 420 and the stock at $44.00—underperformance of approximately 8 percent. Normally this would not be enough to reinstate the buy; however, with the sales remaining very strong we think that our earnings estimates are too low for 1991. We are, therefore, raising our estimates for 1991 to $1.97 a share (from $1.95) and to $2.25 for 1992.

I could go on and on, but you get the idea: One stock's fortunes—good or bad—can affect another's. And it's not all a neat, tidy little formula. Much of the work is deciding what something like a "consumer sentiment survey" really means, if anything.

Watch for more examples of pairs trading in the next two chapters.

As I've said before, my whole investment style depends on having benchmarks. I need to know where the market is trading, how the industries are doing within that framework and how the stocks within each industry are performing against each other. All that was almost impossible during the Crash. The benchmarks were gone. Trading was so frantic, so willy-nilly, that the New York Stock Exchange computers couldn't keep up with the pace. The computerized version of the old-fashioned ticker tape ran as far as two hours behind trades on the floor of the Exchange. By the end of the day, 604 million shares of stock had exchanged hands—nearly triple the volume of a normal trading day.

The delay was bad enough for my pension accounts, the funds I manage for a living. My personal stock portfolio was in such shambles after the Crash that it took days for the Charles Schwab brokerage house to sort out the mess. I didn't know what I had *actually* paid for any of the stocks I bought—or made from stocks I sold—for about a week after the Crash. I didn't even know for sure whether I had even made the trades I thought I made.

All this meant that the investment world was flying without a net. Suppose the ticker tape showed Bristol-Myers selling for $55 a share and Johnson & Johnson selling for $60. It is quite possible that I would have purchased Bristol-Myers and sold Johnson & Johnson—but I wouldn't have known whether that price was two hours old. By the time my trade went through, I might have actually bought Bristol-Myers for $56.50 a share; I might have made a lot less on Johnson & Johnson because its share price might have been lower than I thought. There was no way to know.

And if you were an aggressive investor, there was nothing else you could do.

The one thing you could not do—and many investors did it—was sit there wringing your hands and shaking your head. Too many people did that. A stock market crash could hardly be called a terrific buying opportunity, but there were opportunities to be had. And investors can't find those opportunities by sitting around waiting. They had to act. And the only way to act that day was by the seat of your pants, relying on experience, using what you knew about the stock market instead of fretting over what you did not know about it.

For example: I follow the pharmaceutical industry. I know where drug companies should be trading relative to one another. Suppose I watched five drug stocks on the day of the Crash. If four of them were off 20 percent and one was off 35 percent, then you buy the one that's off 35 percent. That's the one that has the most room to rise if things get better and the least room to fall if things get worse.

For example: Back to Bristol-Myers and Johson & Johnson. I didn't know if the world was coming to an end on October 19, 1987. I didn't know if I'd be standing in line at a soup kitchen the next day, if bread would sell for a nickel a loaf and still be too expensive. I knew nothing about the future. But I knew about the history of these two stocks. And I felt the relationship between these two pairs of stocks would remain about the same regardless of what else was happening in the stock market. I felt the same about a handful of other stocks that I swap in and out of. With Bristol-Myers and Johnson & Johnson, I knew that the market for drugs and health care products had not evaporated in the the last 24 hours, that the management of both companies had not suddenly become corrupt. I knew that both companies had been growing at about 15 percent a year. So I figured I could compare these stocks just as I would before. When one stock seemed to become "cheap," I'd buy it (remember the last chapter?) and when the other would become "expensive," I'd sell it. In the week immediately following the Crash, I must have swapped Johnson & Johnson and Bristol-Myers six times back and forth—each time picking up a few points in profit.

Remember, the only way to judge whether something is cheap, as in a bargain, or just plain cheap is by evaluating those fundamentals. What makes the company tick? What, if anything, has changed? If the answer is nothing and the price looks cheap, buy.

And if the price looks cheap, nothing is wrong with the fundamentals, and the world is crumbling all around you, bid down.

That's what happened when the phone rang and a trader offered to sell 300,000 shares of CPC International, a packaged food company that makes Hellmann's Real Mayonnaise and Knorr soup mixes. It was a company I had owned off and on for much of the 1980s, recently buying back into it at about $40 a share. It was moving up steadily through August. Just two months before the Crash, it was selling at about $56 a share.

When the trader offered this block for $28 a share, I wasn't feeling too well. I had already lost about 25 percent of my fund's value. I figured I had nothing to lose and said, "They can only fire me once."

I offered to buy the whole lot of stock for $27 a share. I bid him down shamelessly, offering a price nobody would take if the scent of panic were not heavy in the air. I could have never gotten away with such insolence on any other day of the century.

By the end of the day, I had made a profit on CPC International. A week later, I had a big profit. A month later it was huge. A year after that, I had doubled my money. My thinking goes back to the fundamentals: If the Crash of '87 was going to plunge the world into darkness, a company that makes mayo and soup is probably going to do better than a company that makes cars, like General

Motors. It seemed like the safest sort of investment you could make under the circumstances.

The point: You can never lose your nerve in investments. Otherwise, you miss the opportunities. I felt this company was going to be okay. I liked it when it was $40 a share, I liked it at $56 a share. I couldn't see any reason not to like it at $27 a share—less than half the price. The thing I could never understand is why somebody else could have owned it and liked it at $56 but turn around and sell it at $27. No matter. I'm glad it happened. It helped turn a dreadful October into a good November.

Again, you could not do nothing. You had to act on what you knew, not sit still because of what you didn't know. And there was a lot you didn't know.

There was no telling how this enormous crash would affect the nation's economy. Everyone knows the Crash of '29 launched the Great Depression in the United States, a depression so severe and so long, it took World War II to end it! Would it happen again? President Reagan, in an interview at the time, said this was just a problem with the stock market, a correction. He didn't know any more than I did. But he was right.

As it turned out, my philosophy was right too.

Of the 19 stocks I bought on October 19 and 20—including CPC International—only 5 had lost money by the end of 1987. A year after that, only one was still in the red—Kinder-Care, and we've been through that story already. The net gain after 2 months was 15 percent; after 14 months, I had made 27 percent on the stocks I bought during history's worst stock market crash (see Figure 12-1).

Stocks purchased Oct. 19–20, 1987

# shares	Stock	Price	12-87 price	Chg.	12-88 price	Chg.
30000	Am. Cyanid	32.23	41.25	28%	46.75	45%
20000	Bristol Meyers	$37.88	41.63	10%	45.25	19%
30000	Emerson Elect.	$27.00	34.63	28%	30.38	13%
10000	Gillette	$29.63	28.38	- 4%	33.25	12%

100000	Halliburton	$27.68	24.75	-11%	28	1%
34400	Quaker Oats	$38.17	41.63	9%	53.12	39%
30000	Telecom "A"	$18.96	23.63	25%	26.12	38%
30000	Union Pacific	$49.38	54	9%	64.25	30%
8400	Wal-Mart	$22.50	26	16%	31.38	39%
50000	Parker Hamilton	$32.50	Sold, 35.88	– –	– –	10%
40000	Browning-Ferris	$21.26	28	32%	27.38	29%
360000	CPC Int'l	$27.00	40.5	50%	51.88	92%
892000	Computer Assoc.	$19.72	32	62%	31.88	62%
20000	Dun & Brandst't	$46.88	54.75	17%	53.63	14%
90000	Kinder-Care	$10.00	8.75	-12%	7.5	-25%
60000	Laidlaw "B"	$10.84	11	1%	14.5	34%
20000	Loews	$68.47	66.63	-3%	78.88	15%
45000	Reuters	$49.63	55.38	12%	56.75	14%
50000	Unocal	$29.26	28.25	-3%	37.88	29%
AVE. CHG				15%		27%

Fig. 12.1

Earlier that year, my firm had bid on several accounts with major corporations and public entities to manage their pension accounts. The process is just like any bidding procedure. The client wants to know how you do what you do and how you measure your success. The clients would ask what do I expect to do. My answer: I expect to beat the Standard & Poor's 500 stock index. Simple as that. Despite losing 25 percent of my fund's value, the market lost more. At the end of 1987, my fund was up 16 percent; the S&P 500 was up 5.3 percent.

For three days during the week after the market crashed on October 19, 1987, the New York Stock Exchange halted trading at 2 P.M. Weary traders and brokers could catch their breath—and catch up on the paperwork that had raced so far ahead of them during that calamitous period.

I just let my hedges grow.

13

Sowing My Oats

Before Michael Jordan retired from the Chicago Bulls, he seemed to be as much of a hotshot on the television screen as he was on the basketball court. You could hardly turn on the TV without seeing Jordan hawking some kind of product, including McDonald's restaurants, Hanes underwear, Nike sneakers, Coca-Cola and Gatorade. All of them doubtless paid handsome royalties to the king of the courts for the privilege of linking his name with their product. From time to time, I have wondered how much better off I'd have been if those companies had saved a little of their money. On the other hand, maybe Michael Jordan had a tiny part in boosting my own success. I'll explain why in a minute.

During the 1980s, while Jordan was helping to drag the Bulls from basketball's basement toward three championship rings, I had the most successful run of investments in my entire career. How did I do it? Did I make successful investment plays in rocket research or high-tech computer technology? Did I figure out a foolproof system for predicting stock market success? Of course not. If you've been reading carefully up to now, you know better. Remember: Invest in what you know. I don't know beans about computers, technology or rocket science. I know beans about beans. And mayonnaise. And baby food and ready-to-eat breakfast cereal and ketchup and pasta. Ask me about food stocks, and I can tell you a little something about what sells and why. The business of the food companies is straightforward. It is something I understand. And yes, the stuff of high finance can truly be made of these simple things.

INSIDE LINE

Don't buy stock in a company in which you can't understand its distribution methods, its products or the way it makes money. If someone has to explain it to you four or five times and you still don't get it, then there's only one thing you really need to understand: Someone is trying to talk you into something.

If you don't invest in something you know and understand, how will you know when to sell it?

Including oatmeal.

If you like oatmeal, chances are pretty good you've heard of a company called Quaker Oats. In fact, you're probably hard pressed to think of any other company that makes oatmeal—that's how overwhelming the Quaker Oats company is. The company owns 60 percent of the hot cereal market worldwide. But the company also has another star performer on its hands—and that's where Michael Jordan comes in. In 1983, Quakers Oats spent a cool $238 million in cash to buy Stokely-Van Camp. Sure, they got the company that makes baked beans and a bunch of other canned foods, but Quaker Oats also got Gatorade, a company that was going nowhere fast. Going nowhere, that is, until they signed on with Michael Jordan and started to market the drink aggressively. Ten years later, Gatorade alone accounted for $.13 of every $1 in Quaker Oats's sales. It had an 89 percent death grip on the sports drink market.

Obviously, I don't want to overstate Michael Jordan's role in my success. Certainly, he helped make Gatorade a popular drink, but Quaker Oats has a reputation for being a good company anyway. I first bought stock in Quaker Oats in late 1983, the year the company bought Stokely-Van Camp. Through the rest of the decade, I probably bought and sold stock in the company more often than I bought any other food company's. Think of Quaker Oats as the backbone for this chapter, a perfect example of a high-quality, good growth company that always makes money—but is not always the best investment. I'll explain what I mean by that in a moment.

In the last chapter, we saw an example of how the p/e ratio formed the benchmark for my investments in a short period of frantic trading during the Crash of 1987. Here, we see how it is sustained over several years of trading in an industry that could virtually do nothing wrong for an entire decade. If you had bought Quaker Oats stock in December 1983, held on to it for almost six years and sold it in June of 1989 as I did, you could have raked in 32.5 percent per year. But consider this: Quaker Oats was just one horse in a race that included many winners.

Kellogg's with its breakfast cereals, Ralston Purina with its cat and dog food, Gerber with its baby foods—all made unbelievable profits and showed soaring growth rates during the mid- to late 1980s. Remember when I said Quaker Oats was always a good *company*, but not always the best *investment?* Here is what I mean: When all the horses are good, you must think of the competition as a tournament, not a single race. Each heat ends with the closing bell every day. One day, one horse may look stronger; the next day, another could lead the pack. The key, of course, is how to tell the difference. That's what we'll talk about in this chapter. But first, some background.

FROM BUST TO BOOM

The packaged food industry took a beating in the '70s and early '80s when raw material prices rose for food companies, but their ability to raise prices in the supermarket didn't. Food pricing power was not sufficient during that period because the poor economy, generally high inflation and pressure from consumers kept food companies from pricing ahead of inflation for a box of cereal.

By 1983, as the economy was emerging from a slump, the fortunes of the food companies improved with the rest of the economy. First, the companies could raise their prices. Once, you paid a dollar for a box of cereal; now, you pay almost five dollars. The cereal is the same. The only difference is the price tag and the face of the athlete on the front of the box. Then, it was Mary Lou Retton and Pete Rose. Now, it's Wayne Gretsky. The consumer was wealthier, times weren't as tough, we had money to spend, we wanted the brand-name goods—so we didn't pay any attention to the rising cost of food. The prices went up, but the cost of raw materials didn't. Food companies were flush with cash.

At the same time, food companies were making better decisions about how they should do business. A company that made the number four or five brand of pasta might decide to get out of the business altogether and sell its pasta division to a competitor. The pages of my stock recommendations tell the story: Beatrice Foods took over Tropicana orange juice in 1979; General Foods acquired Oscar Meyer in 1981; General Mills, which once produced toys and furniture, dumped those divisions at the end of 1985; Ralston Purina got rid of its Jack in the Box restaurants.

In other words, many food companies were sticking with what they knew best and getting rid of what they didn't. If one food company couldn't produce the number one, two or three brand of egg noodles, the company dumped it and concentrated on its more successful product lines.

WHAT TO DO WITH ALL THIS CASH?

Between the lower raw materials costs and the higher prices and the consolidation of product lines, many food companies at this time had more cash than they knew what to do with. Or, to put it more accurately, the bad companies didn't know what to do with it. The good ones did: They bought back their own stock, millions and millions of shares worth of stock. Ralston Purina was the champion of stock buybacks: Between early 1981 and late 1984, the company bought back 25 million shares of its own stock—about 20 percent. By October of 1990, the company had sucked up a total of 62 million shares of its stock, about 53 percent of the total.

Why is that a big deal? And why is that good for investors?

First of all, it's simple supply and demand: At the start of the decade, Ralston had about 118 million shares on the market, available to anyone who wanted to buy them. Ten years later, less than half that number was on the table. There wasn't as much stock out there to buy; it stands to reason that every share was a little more valuable.

But even more important than that, remember what drives investors: earnings per share. Investors want to see good numbers, strong numbers, numbers that increase from year to year. Suppose ABC Foods made a million bucks last year and has a million shares outstanding. ABC made $1 a share. Now suppose the next year, ABC bought back 20 percent of its stock, but it still made $1 million. Suddenly, ABC's earnings per share have increased to $1.25. That's the kind of news investors want to hear.

We heard news like that a lot in the 1980s. CPC International—which makes Hellmann's Mayonnaise, Knorr soup mixes and Thomas' English Muffins—bought back more than a third of its outstanding shares. Heinz bought 4 million shares.

All was good with the world.

MERGER MANIA

Besides the consolidation of product lines among the different companies, there was major consolidation among entire food companies. This was the 1980s; Michael Milken, junk bonds and hostile takeovers were the buzzwords of the decade. So it shouldn't surprise anyone to know that the decade ended with fewer packaged food companies than it had at the start. The largest takeover in history—KKR's takeover of RJR Nabisco—came in 1988 for $25.07 billion. That came after R.J. Reynolds bought Nabisco several years earlier. That year, 1988, also saw Philip Morris buy Kraft for $13.4 billion and Grand Metropolitan buy Pillsbury for $5.7 billion.

The takeover mania created a feeding frenzy among speculators in the food industry, if you'll pardon the expression. Savvy investors knew that anyone who tried to take over ABC Foods, for example, would pay a premium price to existing stockholders in the company. Even rumors about a takeover would increase the price of a company's stock. I benefitted several times.

I bought stock in Esmark—which made Swift meat products, Wesson Oil and Max Factor makeup—in March of 1984. I paid $39.40 a share. Within three months, I had doubled my money. Beatrice Foods took over Esmark by paying $80.00 a share. The story was almost identical with General Foods. I bought stock in the company in June 1985 because I thought it was cheap, and I knew it could be a takeover target; I was right. Five months later, Bird's Eye frozen vegetables, Maxwell House coffee, Jell-O and Post Raisin Bran all became part of Philip Morris. I bought General Foods at $69.50 a share; Philip Morris paid me $120.00 a share— 73 percent profit. Not a bad day's work if you can get it, wouldn't you say?

Buy and Sell Recommendations for Food Stocks

11-8-79	Beatrice	buy
3-19-80	CPC	buy
10-23-80	CPC	buy
2-9-81	Beatrice	buy
3-8-82	Beatrice	hold
3-31-82	General Foods	buy
8-11-82	General Foods	buy
11-19-82	General Mills	buy
12-2-82	CPC	sell
(swap)	General Mills	buy
12-27-83	Quaker Oats	buy
3-12-84	Esmark	buy
4-3-84	Beatrice	buy

(*continued*)

6-27-84	Quaker Oats	sell
8-14-84	Quaker Oats	buy
8-23-84	Quaker Oats	sell
(swap)	Ralston Purina	buy
1-16-85	Quaker Oats	buy
2-14-85	Beatrice	sell
(swap)	Ralston Purina	buy
5-6-85	General Mills	buy
6-4-85	General Foods	buy
7-1-85	General Mills	sell
11-28-85	Quaker Oats	sell
1-14-86	Quaker Oats	buy
3-13-86	Borden	buy
6-16-86	Kellogg	buy
6-27-86	Kellogg	sell
7-2-86	Quaker Oats	sell
11-5-86	CPC	buy
1-6-87	Heinz	buy
3-19-87	Quaker Oats	buy
4-15-87	Borden	sell
4-21-87	Pillsbury	sell
(swap)	CPC	buy
5-5-87	General Mills	buy
9-4-87	Heinz	sell
4-7-88	Quaker Oats	buy
6-8-88	General Mills	sell
10-20-88	Ralston Purina	sell
1-9-89	Gerber	buy
6-6-89	Quaker Oats	sell
12-15-89	CPC	buy
2-9-90	Heinz	buy
3-12-90	Heinz	sell
6-28-90	Gerber	sell
8-6-90	Gerber	buy
10-29-90	Ralston Purina	buy
11-7-90	Borden	buy
1-4-91	Borden	sell
2-1-91	Borden	sell
2-5-91	Gerber	sell
7-9-91	Gerber	buy
8-23-91	Ralston Purina	sell
(swap)	Warner Lambert	buy
9-24-91	Gerber	sell
1-30-92	CPC	buy
3-17-92	CPC	sell

Making Hay with Oats (and Others)

So what does any of this have to do with Quaker Oats?

Well, not all our food stock investments were quite so profitable in such a short time. The fact is, we have so far only explained the environment that we met when we decided to begin investing heavily in food stocks in 1983. At the time, I worked with a stock analyst whom I considered a genius, Alan Greditor. He and I saw this series of events coming together to make the packaged food industry a feast of an investment opportunity. By the time it was all over, I had become known in the investment community as the "king of the food stocks," owning two to three times as much in food companies as any other institutional investor. As much as 8 percent of my portfolio was devoted to food stocks—a whopping figure when you consider how many thousands of companies in dozens of industries could get a piece of my investment pie.

To explain some of that success and how we managed our food stock portfolio, Quaker Oats seems like a logical choice to anchor the story. Eleven times in a six-year period, I recommended either selling or buying stock in the company.

Throughout the entire decade, you can see when I favored Quaker Oats or when I preferred other food companies, simply by plotting out the dates of our buy and sell recommendations in a list. This is not a comprehensive list of every food stock I bought or sold, or every company I traded. It is a good list of some of the major recommendations on companies I was most concerned with.

In an earlier chapter, we spent a bit of time discussing the p/e ratio and why it is so important to the work I do. It gives us a benchmark to measure a stock's performance against other stocks and the market as a whole. A p/e ratio doesn't help much unless you have something to compare it to—and you know where the p/e historically is for a company or for the market. To understand what I mean, let's look at the first food stock purchase listed on the previous page: Beatrice Foods. This buy recommendation came four years before we heavily bought into the packaged food industry.

Timeline on Quaker Oats (Oat)

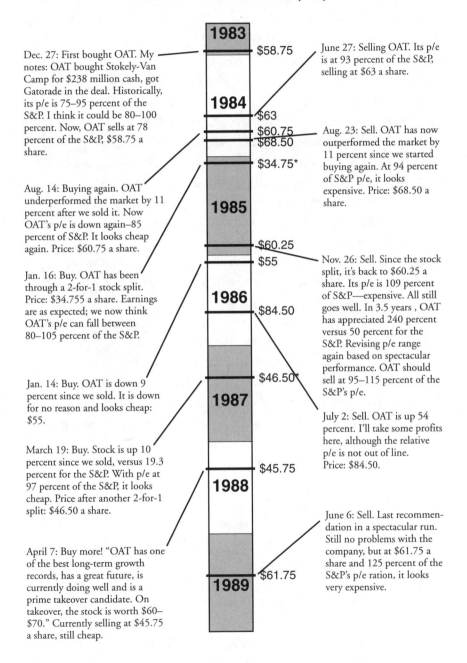

1983

Dec. 27: First bought OAT. My notes: OAT bought Stokely-Van Camp for $238 million cash, got Gatorade in the deal. Historically, its p/e is 75–95 percent of the S&P. I think it could be 80–100 percent. Now, OAT sells at 78 percent of the S&P, $58.75 a share.

$58.75

June 27: Selling OAT. Its p/e is at 93 percent of the S&P, selling at $63 a share.

1984

$63
$60.75
$68.50
$34.75*

Aug. 14: Buying again. OAT underperformed the market by 11 percent after we sold it. Now OAT's p/e is down again–85 percent of S&P. It looks cheap again. Price: $60.75 a share.

Aug. 23: Sell. OAT has now outperformed the market by 11 percent since we started buying again. At 94 percent of S&P p/e, it looks expensive. Price: $68.50 a share.

1985

Jan. 16: Buy. OAT has been through a 2-for-1 stock split. Price: $34.755 a share. Earnings are as expected; we now think OAT's p/e can fall between 80–105 percent of the S&P.

$60.25
$55

Nov. 26: Sell. Since the stock split, it's back to $60.25 a share. Its p/e is 109 percent of S&P—expensive. All still goes well. In 3.5 years , OAT has appreciated 240 percent versus 50 percent for the S&P. Revising p/e range again based on spectacular performance. OAT should sell at 95–115 percent of the S&P's p/e.

1986

$84.50

Jan. 14: Buy. OAT is down 9 percent since we sold. It is down for no reason and looks cheap: $55.

$46.50*

1987

March 19: Buy. Stock is up 10 percent since we sold, versus 19.3 percent for the S&P. With p/e at 97 percent of the S&P, it looks cheap. Price after another 2-for-1 split: $46.50 a share.

July 2: Sell. OAT is up 54 percent. I'll take some profits here, although the relative p/e is not out of line. Price: $84.50.

$45.75

1988

June 6: Sell. Last recommendation in a spectacular run. Still no problems with the company, but at $61.75 a share and 125 percent of the S&P's p/e ration, it looks very expensive.

April 7: Buy more! "OAT has one of the best long-term growth records, has a great future, is currently doing well and is a prime takeover candidate. On takeover, the stock is worth $60–$70." Currently selling at $45.75 a share, still cheap.

$61.75

1989

Fig. 13.1

Quaker Oats was an incredible success story during the nearly six years I swapped in and out of it, but it wasn't the only one. I owned stock in a dozen different packaged food companies at the same time, sometimes switching out of OAT and into others when the time was right. Between my first buy recommendation and my last sell recommendation, the stock's price more than tripled—but that doesn't really describe my success. Presumabbly, I wasn't around when OAT was down; I was investing in OTHER food stocks!

In an earlier chapter, we spent a bit of time discussing the p/e ratio and why it is so important to the work I do. It gives us a bench-mark to measure a stock's performance against other stocks and the market as a whole. A p/e ratio doesn't help much unless you have something to compare it to—and you know where the o/e histori-cally is for a company or for the market. To understand what I mean, let's look at the first food stock purchase listed on the previous page: Beatrice Foods. This buy recommendation came four years before we heavily bought into the packaged food industry.

On November 8, 1979, I recommended the company, one month after I started to work at SunBank. The recommendation is still in my files, complete with a list of products the company produced: Dannon Yogurt, La Choy oriental food, Eckrich cold cuts and Tropicana. Each stock recommendation sheet includes the current stock price, its recent earnings-per-share figures, its price/earnings ratio and, of course, comparable figures for the stock market's Standard & Poor's index.

As part of our analysis, we compare the p/e of the company with the p/e of the S&P. In this case, for example, the 1979 p/e ratio for Beatrice was 7.0—the stock price was 7 times its earnings. For the market, the p/e was 7.5 times earnings. That means Beatrice was selling at about 93 percent of the Standard & Poor's average—7.0 is 93 percent of 7.5. The next year, 1980, Beatrice's p/e ratio was only 6.5, while the S&P index's p/e ratio was 8.2. Beatrice was sell-ing at only 79 percent of the S&P average. That only becomes meaningful when you know more about Beatrice. And if you've tracked a company for many years with this sort of analysis, you'll know more about the company. Here's the key part of the stock recommendation: "Over the past many years, Beatrice has sold between 87 percent and 130 percent of the S&P average, well above current levels. It is felt that between 85 percent and 100 percent is a reasonable range and one that should yield above average appreciation." In plain English: Beatrice is selling at a discount right now. It looks cheap compared to the market as a whole. It would cost you less to buy a dollar's worth of earnings from Beatrice than from the S&P index. Beatrice is on sale. Buy it.

This relationship is key. It assumes, of course, that you have already considered any other factors that could affect a stock: The management is sound, the products are good, the marketing techniques are valid, the competition isn't plotting any surprises. It assumes, all other things being equal, that a stock should sell at a certain level relative to the rest of the stock market. When it's selling at a level (relative to the market) below those expectations, it's cheap. And when it strengthens and reaches the top limits of those expectations, it sells at a premium to the market. It has probably reached the top of its ladder; perhaps it's time to find another ladder to climb.

This begins to explain what I meant earlier when I said Quaker Oats could be a good company, but not always a good investment. Let's explain that more by skipping ahead a few years. You can see I dabbled some in food stocks, before the fire really caught on in the packaged food industry. When I first recommended Quaker Oats at the end of 1983, the stock sold at $58.75 a share. It had just purchased Stokely-Van Camp (with Gatorade), and its projected p/e ratio was only 78 percent of the market. Historically, the company had done better than that before, selling as high as 95 percent of the market multiple; we thought it could do even better.

INSIDE LINE

Do keep your portfolio fresh. As you can see in this chapter, I do not hang on to stocks very long if there are better investment opportunities to be had. In fact, I have an annual turnover rate of 100 percent in my portfolio. I usually don't hold on to a stock for more than one year because I am constantly trading one company for an-other, as we're discussing here.

I don't necessarily recommend that kind of turnover for an individual investor. But no turnover, or only 10 percent or 20 per-cent turnover, is too low. Keep your portfolio fresh because com-panies are always changing. There's nothing wrong with 50 percent turnover every year.

Six months later to the day, we issued another recommenda-tion on Quaker Oats. The fact is, nothing had really changed; the June 1984 stock recommendation sheet in my files is a photocopy of the December 1983 recommendation. The only differences: The price of the stock and the substance of the advice. The price had climbed $4.25 a share—we made money. But it was time to sell the stock.

Why? The company still made Flako pie crusts, Aunt Jemima syrup and Celeste frozen pizzas. I didn't expect anyone to stop buy-ing those foods; I certainly didn't think anything was wrong with the company. So why dump a stock that was performing like a thor-oughbred?

Remember, when the stock price went up, that also affected Quaker Oats's p/e ratio (price of the stock divided by earnings). If we plot the numbers (price, earnings per share, p/e and p/e relative to the market) on a chart, here's how it would have looked in December 1983:

	Price	*EPS*	*P/E*	*P/E Relative to S&P*
OAT	$58.75	$6.70	8.7	.78
S&P	$185.10	$16.50	11.2	1.00

Follow the chart across: When we decided to buy Quaker Oats, the price was $58.75 a share on earnings of $6.70 a share. Divide 58.75 by 6.70 and that translates to a p/e ratio of 8.7, or 78 percent of the S&P index. Again, at the time, that looked like a bargain.

Now, here was the situation six months later:

	Price	EPS	P/E	P/E Relative to S&P
OAT	$63.00	$6.70	9.4	.93
S&P	$173.00	$17.15	10.1	1.00

Quaker Oats's price had gone up; the earnings per share had not yet had time to change. That means the p/e ratio rose to 9.4. At the same time, the price of the S&P dropped, earnings rose and the p/e ratio dropped slightly. Suddenly, Quaker Oats was looking less like a bargain. We expected the stock to sell at about 95 percent of the market. Guess what? We're almost at the upper end of Quaker Oats's range. Time to sell and find something that looks a little cheaper. At the time, we had already begun to move on to something else. As the earlier food chart shows, we bought Beatrice and Esmark, the company that was taken over a few months later, doubling my money.

We sold out of Quaker Oats at the right time. The price dropped nearly three dollars a share before things changed and a good *company* again looked like a good *investment*. Just two months later, here is the chart on Quaker Oats and the market as a whole:

	Price	EPS	P/E	P/E Relative to S&P
OAT	$60.75	$6.52	9.3	.85
S&P	$186.93	$17.15	10.9	1.00

In that two-month period, you'll notice that the market performed like gangbusters while Quaker Oats slipped. We certainly noticed it: "OAT has underperformed the market by 11 percent since we moved it to a 'sell' on June 27, 1984. Fiscal year 1984 earnings per share came in on schedule at $6.52. The stock sells at the low end of a 78–98 percent relative p/e range."

There are a couple of key items to note in that statement. First, I've said before that earnings drive the market. We expected earnings of $6.70 a share; we got earnings of $6.52, just about what we expected. Second, the p/e range where we expected Quaker Oats to perform relative to the S&P didn't change much. What changed was the market's performance next to the Quaker Oats. Now, the company looks like a bargain again because *the cost of a dollar's worth of earnings is near the bottom of its range relative to the market as a whole.*

Again, things didn't take long to change. Within 10 days of our buy recommendation, Quaker Oats's price skyrocketed nearly $8.00 a share. Its p/e ratio slammed into the top of its range and it was time to swap into something that looked a little bit cheaper. Our choice was Ralston Purina.

	Price	*EPS*	*P/E*	*P/E Relative to S&P*
OAT	$68.50	$6.52	10.5	.94
S&P	$189.20	$17.15	11.0	1.00
RAL	$29.50	$2.93	10.1	.92

Cheaper, as you recall, is a relative term. Obviously, one share of Ralston Purina costs less than a share of Quaker Oats, but that's not what makes it cheaper. Ralston had cash to spend. It was buying back millions of shares of its own stock. Its raw material costs were down, and its pet food prices were up 3.5 percent since June, two months earlier. We expected its p/e ratio to be between 88 percent and 100 percent of the Standard & Poor's p/e ratio. It looked like Ralston had some room for its stock price to rise; Quaker Oats didn't. The company was at the top of its range compared to the market.

Five months and a stock split later, Quaker Oats was a bargain again.

INSIDE LINE

What's a stock split?

In simple terms, a stock split gives investors more shares of a company at a lower price. For example, suppose you owned 100 shares of ABC Widget Co. at $50 a share. If the company decided on a 2-for-1 stock split, you'd end up with 200 shares of the company at $25 a share. Typically, this is done when the price of a single share gets so high, the company thinks it might discourage investors from buying. By splitting, the price per share drops for anyone who wants to buy in, and existing shareholders get more shares.

A company could call for other ratios in a stock split. A 3-for-2 split, for example, would turn those 100 shares into 150 shares, each worth $33.33. A split does not change the value of your holdings—only the way they are distributed.

The stock was now selling for $34.75 a share (half what it was before—but we owned twice as much), and its p/e ratio was about the same as usual. Now, however, thanks to Oats's strong showing in the past few months, we upped its range a little. We decided the company could probably perform a little stronger next to the market, so we set its range between 80 percent and 105 percent of the S&P average. (Remember, p/e ratios are not static. People will pay more if the company has a better outlook.) That meant Quaker Oats was no longer at the top of its range. Here's how the chart looked this time:

	Price	EPS	P/E	P/E Relative to S&P
OAT	$34.75	$3.75	9.30	.93
S&P	$191.80	$19.20	10.00	1.00

We could continue with this for the rest of the decade, but you probably get the idea: Only invest in a stock when it seems to have room to improve. My investment strategy depends heavily on knowing what a stock is *worth*, what it *ought* to be able to sell for. That's where the p/e comes in and why it is so important to compare a company's p/e with this historic range and the Standard & Poor's index. Consider this: After our buy recommendation on Quaker Oats in January of 1985, we revisited the stock *again* in November of the same year. What did we have to say for ourselves? "As with other food stocks, OAT has had a spectacular run in the last 3.5 years, appreciating some 240 percent versus 50 percent for the S&P. Since January, OAT is up 73 percent versus 16 percent for the S&P." The stock was selling at a 9 percent premium to the S&P index. The stock price had soared to $60.25. Its p/e had scaled to nearly the top of its range. It was time to take our profits and find another company that had more room at the top.

This strategy is the key to pairs trading, playing one stock off another. When one stock is expensive, sell it and find one that's cheap. Obviously, we would like to see our stocks do nothing but appreciate. When we buy it, we expect to be buying it near the bottom and we expect to hold it until it tops out. I won't beat around the bush: I'm proud of how we were able to ride food stocks up by jumping from one to the other throughout the decade. My recommendations are full of swaps from one company that showed some weakness to another that showed some strength.

In early 1985, for example, we dumped Beatrice Foods in favor of Ralston Purina. Beatrice sold at about 97 percent of the S&P 400; Ralston sold at about 92 percent of the market. Ralston had more "upside" than Beatrice, the company was better managed, it had more cash (remember all those stock buybacks?) and it was an easy recommendation: "Ralston is a superior company to Beatrice in every possible way, yet it sells at a slight p/e discount. SWITCH!" We first bought Ralston when it sold at $29.50 a share. By the time we decided to sell the stock for the last time, it went for $85.40 a share—almost triple what we'd first paid for it.

Still, the best illustration of how explosive this phenomenal food stock boom could be was my 11-day affair with the Kellogg Company. The company is the most famous breakfast food maker in the world. It is certainly the largest, commanding 50 percent of the ready-to-eat cereal market worldwide and 38 percent of the market in the United States. For 34 years (before mid-1986), Kellogg had an unbroken streak of record earnings. On June 16, 1986, we issued a buy recommendation on the stock, noting that it was an extremely well-run company, but that for some reason its stock looked cheap. Here's how the chart looked for Kellogg at the time:

	Price	*EPS*	*P/E*	*P/E Relative to S&P*
K	$47.25	$2.60	18.2	1.16
S&P	$275.50	$17.50	15.7	1.00

Historically, Kellogg had sold between a 90 percent discount to the market and a 130 percent premium to the market. With the food industry having such a heyday, we estimated that the company could do even better, trading between 110 percent and 125 percent of the market. You'll notice in the right-hand column of the chart that Kellogg is closer to the bottom of that range. We bought it.

On June 27, 11 days later, we reversed. Tony the Tiger (and his company) were still great. The stock price had just gotten ahead of itself: "Kellogg is up 20.6 percent since our June 16 buy recommendation versus 1.1 percent for the S&P. It has exceeded our original target." Here's the chart:

	Price	*EPS*	*P/E*	*P/E Relative to S&P*
K	$57.00	$2.60	21.9	1.34
S&P	$278.60	$17.00	16.4	1.00

Remember my advice from an earlier chapter: Buy cheap, sell expensive.

END OF AN ERA

Earlier, I said I was proud of how we rode this wave as high as it could go. We used our heads; when a stock became too expensive, we didn't let our guts rule us. We didn't hang on to a stock because it had been good to us or because we thought the stock deserved a longer ride. We sold out and moved on to something that looked like it could grow.

I am equally proud of the fact that, when the circumstances of the economy changed and the fortunes of the food companies started to wane, we saw that coming too. We sold out completely at exactly the right time.

By 1990, it was coming to an end. The '87 crash had dried up much of the takeover activity. Michael Milken's crown had tarnished. The go-go years of the economy were winding down. There was very little room for consolidation within the packaged food industry. At one time, 8 percent of my portfolio was devoted to food stocks; that diminished to about 2 percent by the time I wrote in a 1991 recommendation to sell Gerber, "The market hates food stocks."

Throughout the decade, I enjoyed the successes of these food companies, but I could never figure out why Quaker Oats would benefit so much from Gatorade. I tried it after a round of golf once. It was awful. I don't know how you could say to someone with a straight face, "This is a great product." I guess it's a good thing I didn't try it before I invested in Quaker Oats. I would have repeated my experience with the cookie wars.

CHANGE IS IN THE WIN

Okay, so I'm not the greatest golfer in the world. I have a 14 handicap, I'm perfectly capable of three-putting a hole and I won't wager more than a golf tee on my game. I'm not even improving.

But I know enough about the game to know when it's changing. A few years ago, the latest in golf technology came out—the Big Bertha line of clubs from Callaway Golf. I watched fellow hackers grab these clubs and knock their balls farther than I'd ever seen them hit before. Where Ping had once dominated the sport with its line of golf clubs, a newcomer was sweeping the links. Callaway created woods with shafts that plunged all the way to the bottom of the club head, giving golfers more power. They invented the "HeavenWood," a seven-wood utility club with an inch longer shaft (and better distance). These were the new hot clubs, and everyone wanted a piece of the action—including me. I bought my Big Bertha driver and "HeavenWood" and I loved them.

Change excites investors too, as long as it's the right kind of change. The packaged food industry underwent a major shift in the 1980s and I was fortunate enough to grab the coattails and hang on for the ride. Prices rose. Companies consolidated their product lines. Major corporations merged or bought out competitors. All this change added up to a period of phenomenal profit making in the food industry. That's what investors are looking for.

As I write this, people aren't taking over food companies anymore. They're buying up banks. We expected giant consolidation in the banking industry, similar to what we found in packaged foods. We found banks that were likely takeover targets and put our money in them, making a few dollars here and there along the way. Remember, taking over a company means someone usually has to pay shareholders a big premium. If the stock market puts XYZ Bank at $50 a share, another bank will probably have to pay $60-plus to buy up enough stock to finish the deed. We found that Florida, Arizona, New Jersey, Virginia and the New England region were fertile ground for bank mergers and takeovers.

There have been other changes in line for banks as well. In 1992–93, interest rates hit record lows. Consumers wanted loans. The spread is larger between what banks pay for money and what they charge for it (the discount rate versus the prime rate, etc.). Banks can make more money. Additionally, as consumers cash in those low-paying certificates of deposit and hunt for a place to invest the money, a lot of banks are moving into areas that have traditionally remained outside their marble walls: mutual funds, for example.

We started playing these changes in their infancy, in the early to mid-1980s. The stocks were cheap and banking was recovering from a rough decade in the 1970s. The money came fairly easily at the time. For example, we first recommended Florida National Bank in August of 1984. The stock was cheap, selling at about 85 percent of the market for $12.62 a share (this is corrected for a stock split). That was fairly cheap at the time for bank stocks, but the bigger attraction is found in the text of the recommendation: Florida National was due to merge with the massive Chemical Bank. Another corporation eventually bought Florida Bank. We watched the stock price rise and doubled our money in two years.

The story is similar with Bank of Boston at the start of 1986. We recommended the stock when it sold for $29.13 a share (adjusted for a 2-for-1 stock split) and a big discount to the market. The company's p/e ratio was about 51 percent that of the market as a whole, significantly cheaper than other bank stocks that were selling at 90 percent of the market. (Remember the translation here: Bank of Boston's p/e ratio was about half that of the market; many other banks had higher p/e ratios and were more expensive relative to the market.) Ten months later, Bank of Boston's stock price was up 46 percent, and it looked like it had reached the top of its relative p/e range. We sold and took the profits.

By the end of 1986, our excitement in that wave of change in the banking industry waned. We sold out of the group and moved on. Between the middle of 1980 and the start of 1987, I traded in 22 different bank stocks. I never held one longer than two and a half years. Some I bought and sold within three months. Returns ranged between 13 percent and 108 percent (except for one Ohio bank that lost 27 percent in 28 months—whoops!) We used the same methods in banking that we used in foods: Watch the changes, anticipate the mergers, monitor those p/e ratios and the value of those stocks. Which ones look cheap?

The wave of changes seemed to return to banking again in 1991. Within a year, we probably owned stock in 15 different banks. We stayed heavily weighted in banking until mid-1993, when we sold about a third of them. It's too soon to tell whether it's a good idea to hold the rest, although as I write this, I suspect we won't stay in banking too long. It's just not the sort of long-term growth industry I like, but I love to trade them when they're coming into vogue.

It is very rewarding when you can find industries that are changing, particularly if you can find them changing for the better. That's where the real money is made. But if you catch them changing for the worse, that's okay too. Remember to sell, not buy. And don't be tempted to bottom-fish—groping for the lowest priced stocks in the barrel. They generally stay down for a long time.

Oh, and speaking of change, Callaway Golf became a public company a full year before I knew anything about its golf-bag Excalibers, the Big Bertha line. The stock had already doubled. After I bought my driver and my HeavenWood, the stock quadrupled—but I had missed my chance to profit. Who knows how well I would have done if I had owned the clubs before the company went public?

14

To Your Health

Think back a few years. Think back before California cuisine became the rage, before anyone had heard of tofu, before "60 Minutes" featured red wine as an antidote to blocked arteries. In the late 1970s, before the exercise craze and the health food craze, nobody had ever heard of cholesterol—least of all me. Not that I was concerned about my health. I have always eaten well and gotten enough exercise to stay trim. I don't smoke or drink. But when the 1980s started, I started to care a great deal about cholesterol and coronary disease and high blood pressure and blemished skin and insomnia—just about any ailment you can think of that could be relieved with a pill, ointment or liquid.

The 1980s were the decade of the drug companies.

It didn't take long for the drug companies to hear about cholesterol. In a 10- to 12-year period, they must have come out with half a dozen different drugs designed to reduce the level of "bad" cholesterol in our arteries and convert it into "good" cholesterol. The laboratories of these pharmaceutical powerhouses churned out drugs with names that sounded like a cast list from a *Star Trek* movie: Merck had its Mevacor, and later Zocor; Squibb had its Pravachol; a division of American Home Products came out with Atromid S; Upjohn had Colestid; and Merrill-Dow had Lorelco.

And these, of course, were just the cholesterol drugs. The 1980s were boom time for the drug companies, which had their best decade for new drug development. For them, it was a time of big growth and mammoth profits. Their earnings grew at rates of 15 percent to 20 percent a year. Pill prices were rising 8 percent a year for seemingly no reason at all—just because the companies could get away with it.

Obviously, it was a boon to my work as well. First of all, the excitement in the pharmaceutical trade gave me something to talk about at insufferable cocktail parties thrown by brokerage houses and other investors. Spend some time watching the foibles and fortunes of the drug companies, and you get to know a little something about the drugs they're producing and what they're supposed to do. If I'm talking to a doctor, I love being able to throw out the name of a new treatment for angina even before the Food and Drug Administration has approved it.

More important, of course, was the opportunity to catch a rising star, as we did with the packaged food industry in the same period. The difference in this case, however, is that I didn't get out in time. With foods, we knew when to start investing, and we knew when the story had played itself out. We left with plenty of time to spare. With health care and drug company stocks, we played the top drug stocks against each other just as we had with food stocks, but we were a little late bailing out—thanks, in part, to the election of Bill Clinton, who publicized the problems without ever increasing the health care budget.

BEGINNING AT THE BEGINNING

Drug companies have always been an investment staple in anyone's portfolio. I was no exception. It wasn't hard to buy into that group of stocks. Pharmaceuticals had been high-growth stocks in the '60s and early '70s. Their growth slowed down in the later '70s and early '80s with a lull in the introduction of new drugs, but you could see that new ones were in the pipeline, ready to be released any time. At the same time, prices started to rise. The doctor prescribed a $1.60 pill for whatever ailed you. A year later, you'd pay $1.80 a pill. The next year, it was up to $2. The reason: You and I didn't pay for it. The drug companies stuck it to consumers, but nobody cared. Our employer's insurance picked up the tab. Add to that the ease of getting new drugs approved, and you see why it was the industry's heyday.

The industry was an easy one to like. With drug companies lining up to introduce new drugs and price increases coming on the old ones, the stage was set for an exciting time in the industry. The situation was very similar to that of the packaged food group. Every company had the potential to be strong. They were all large corporations, reasonably well managed and inventive. It was just a question of whether you would own Merck (the grand poobah of drug companies) or Pfizer or Bristol-Myers.

I traded Bristol-Myers against Johnson & Johnson many times, for example, using the same *modus operandi* as with foods: Are both companies comparable in size and growth rate? What are their p/e ratios? How do those p/e ratios compare to the Standard & Poor's 500 index? Is one selling at a discount? If you're paying attention and monitoring the stocks you're interested in, you can see when one gets ahead of another. Your goal, as always, is to find the companies with the misplaced worth. The market says it's worth one thing, you think it's worth another. If you're right (remember, I'm only right about 55 percent of the time), then the stock will come up to the level you expect.

Clearly, we don't want to spend too much time rehashing the chapter on the packaged food industry. That was a detailed description of my method of comparing the value of two companies in a similar industry and finding the ones that are "cheap." While the philosphy is the same here and we will no doubt run across similar examples, I'd prefer to take some snapshots from my experience with drug stocks and see what investment advice we might find.

REALITY VERSUS PERCEPTION

In some ways, this is a saying we have repeated throughout this book. What seems to be happening in the stock market is often as important as what actually happens. Image is everything. Example: Earnings *estimates* matter as much as the actual earnings. If an analyst holed away in some Manhattan office tower lowers the estimate on ABC Widget's earnings, it spells trouble for ABC's stock. Another example: I might buy a stock when things look bleak (remember The Home Depot a few chapters ago), because I don't really think things are as bleak as they seem.

Usually, the perception is *better* than the reality.

That turned out to be the case with Syntex, a popular pharmaceutical company that has seen success rise and fall like the tides. As a pioneer in the development of birth control pills in the 1960s, the company enjoyed wild growth and popularity, with its stock selling sometimes extremely high, p/e ratios far above the S&P and very, very expensive. As questions started arising about the side effects of birth control pills, the company's stock fell sharply. Then, in 1972, the company introduced its first big blockbuster drug, Naprosyn, an arthritis pain reliever. Twenty years after the drug was invented, Naprosyn and Syntex's sister pain killer called Anaprox made up nearly half the company's $2 billion sales.

In 1983, we were still 10 years away from a critical juncture in the life of Syntex's blockbuster products. At that time, the company's patent on Naprosyn would expire, meaning anyone on earth could apply for approval and start producing and selling it a lot cheaper.

That would cut sharply into Syntex's sales—and, of course, its earnings. We were confident the company was properly preparing for that time because the Syntex laboratories were busily working to crank out four new drugs, each with the potential to be blockbusters in their own right.

As I said earlier, we looked down the pipeline to see what drugs were coming to help us gauge which companies looked strong in the future. For our money, Syntex looked like a good bet: We estimated earnings to be as high as $6 a share with a p/e ratio of 15 that year. That meant the stock could sell for $90 a share in three years—67 percent higher than it was selling that day. The recommendation: Buy Syntex as fast as you can.

A year later, the stock had dropped 21 percent. That alone would not have shooed us off. But a stock doesn't lose one-fifth of its value in a vacuum. The story had changed: Earnings had dropped 40 percent; sales of diagnostic equipment, another arm of Syntex's business, were down. The new drugs we so eagerly expected were delayed until late 1986 or early 1987. When the story changes for the worse, find somewhere else to put your money.

Jump ahead another year, to mid-1986. The picture has become rosy again: "Syntex has one of the best lines of new products for the rest of the decade. This, combined with the recovery of diagnostics, could generate 15 percent growth over the next five years." The stock was selling at less than a 1 percent premium to the market. We expected it to sell for more; we bought. And we were right. At the end of 1986, the stock had jumped 74 percent, and it still looked cheap compared to the market. We repeated our buy recommendation.

And Syntex had not yet released a single new drug.

In fact, the company had just had a minor setback when the Food and Drug Administration did not approve Cardene, Syntex's new drug to treat heart pain from angina. The FDA wanted more information; the move wasn't fatal. But it pushed back the release of new drugs.

By the end of 1987, we had expected to see Cardene on the market. We had also expected to see Ticlid, a drug that helps prevent strokes, and Toradol, a pain relief drug. The next year, we were awaiting Cytovene, a treatment for illnesses caused by virus, and Synarel, a treatment for women with endometriosis. That's what we expected. But in November of 1987, we saw none of it and still, we were optimistic about Syntex. Not that we didn't have good reason. Company earnings had grown 38 percent in 1986 and 29 percent in 1987. The stock was still cheap. The pipeline was still full of promising new drugs. The company had extra cash and was buying back its own stock. We repeated our buy recommendation again that month. When the stock jumped 25 percent in the next 14 months, we decided to take some of the profits and look elsewhere for a while.

The pattern continued for another two years into 1990, when finally, finally, the company got approval for and started releasing some of the drugs on which we had pinned so much faith—Cardene and Cytovene in 1989, Synarel and an injectable version of Toradol in 1990. Ticlid came out in 1991. Early in 1990, we were convinced that Syntex had shed its reputation as a "one-drug company" that relied entirely on Naprosyn for its success.

The result?

This is the result, from our August 1992 sell recommendation: "Some of the new drugs intended to replace the company's mainstays (Naprosyn and Anaprox) have been highly disappointing. . . . Toradol can cause gastrointestinal bleeding." In short, sales for these "blockbuster" drugs fell far below our expectations. In 1990, for example, we estimated sales for Ticlid to reach as high as $300 million in one year—second only to Naprosyn. By 1992, we estimated only $10 million in sales that year with a peak of $50 million in the mid-1990s. And just to rub salt in the wound, the FDA refused in 1993 to approve Syntex's over-the-counter version of Naprosyn—a last-ditch effort to blow new life into an old drug.

"This once-great recommendation has fallen hard this year. Since our April 1990 buy recommendation, Syntex is up 18 percent versus 27 percent for the market," I wrote in the sell rec-ommendation. The illusion was shattered. The reality had caught up with the perception. We took the money and ran. This time the perception was wrong. On to the next idea.

MAKING THE MOST OF A BAD SITUATION

Of all the drug companies, few make as many products you and I recognize as Johnson & Johnson. Is there a household in America that hasn't had Band-Aid bandages in the medicine cabinet? Is there anyone in the country who hasn't been sprinkled with Johnson's Baby Powder or lathered with Johnson's Baby Shampoo at least once? Or popped a pair of Tylenol on a particularly bad day at the office? I'd be amazed to hear otherwise.

In its 100-year-plus history, the company has never posted a loss. It certainly was among the strongest companies in my portfolio, off and on, during this heyday period of drug stocks. While Johnson & Johnson is best known for its over-the-counter consumer prod-ucts and medicines, it also has a sizable prescription drug division. I swapped between Johnson & Johnson and Bristol-Myers fre-quently. In Johnson's case, we expected the stock to trade between 110 percent and 125 percent of the market multiple. In other words, we expected the p/e for Johnson to be at least 10 percent to 25 percent higher than the p/e for the Standard & Poor's 500 index. When it traded at the bottom, we bought; when it traded too high and looked expensive, we sold.

By March of 1985, the news of the day might have scared away some investors who looked at Johnson & Johnson. The company had taken a number of sucker punches in the three or four years prior. First, Procter & Gamble and Kimberly Clark clobbered Johnson's when it tried to pry its way into the disposable baby diaper market. The company cried uncle in 1981, pulling the product from the shelves and giving up. Two years later, in 1983, Johnson & Johnson was forced to pull its antiarthritis drug Zomax off the shelves when the drug was linked to the death of five people.

The biggest blow came in 1982, when eight people died from cyanide-laced capsules of Tylenol in the Chicago area. The company responded with a textbook example of good public relations, recalling 31 million bottles of the product, repackaging the medicine to prevent further tampering and advertising all its efforts to ensure public safety. The campaign cost the company $240 million and cut Tylenol's profits in half.

Through it all, the company showed no change in its earnings per share, the most important statistic a public company has to offer. Earnings didn't increase, but they didn't fall either. As I wrote in the March 1985 recommendation, "To hold earnings per share flat in the face of all this is remarkable."

This is a classic example of a stock market truism: When a piece of bad news comes out about your stock, expect more, because it is very rare that you'll hear only one piece of bad news—or good news for that matter. When the bad news starts coming, stand back; there's sure to be more. But remember this too: Nobody rings a bell to tell you the bottom has arrived. You need to be paying attention to all the other signs and see for yourself when the bulk of the bad news has come out.

In this case, has anything really changed? Were distraught mothers hosing their children down, spraying away any vestige of baby shampoo? Of course not. The *fundamentals* of the company hadn't changed. The only things I cared about were the earnings (impressive, under the circumstances) and the relative value of Johnson & Johnson's stock. Selling at $39.50 a share and a modest premium to the market, the price was a bargain. We bought it with a bushel basket. Nine months later, the price was up to $52.25 a share—up 32 percent, twice as much as the market. The stock was selling closer to the top of its p/e range. The company's decision to stop making disposable diapers was clinical and efficient in the face of tough market competition. So was our decision to sell Johnson & Johnson stock. For now, something else looked cheaper.

KNOW WHEN TO FOLD 'EM

The market has a lot to say. It knows quite a bit and gives hints almost every day about what it's doing and where it's going. Still, there is one thing the market doesn't know: What *you* paid for *your* stock. In fact, the market not only doesn't know what you paid, but it doesn't even care! So when I'm wrong (about 45 percent of the time), it's important that I know when to recognize that. When I'm beaten by a bad story or a bad economy, I have to know when to gather my marbles and go home.

Knowing which stocks to *buy*, and when to buy them, is a learned skill that is obviously very important. But it won't make a bit of difference unless you also know how to *sell* that stock. The only way you can realize your gain is when you sell. And, of course, if you don't sell, then you don't have any money to buy your next idea. Not enough investors are honest with others (and themselves) on this point. Too few will say, "I'm good at buying stock, but I'm terrible at selling." That's not usually one of my problems. As I said in an earlier chapter, I sell most stocks in my portfolio at least once in a year's time. I have 100 percent turnover—very high for any investor and not recommended for most. Everything in my portfolio is for sale at any time—for the right price. And sometimes, just sometimes, the right price isn't as much as I paid for it.

In early 1986, in the midst of the health care and drug company decade, I had invested off and on in Baxter Labs, a hospital supply company. The company had just merged with a competitor, American Hospital, and the short-term effect on its balance sheet was disastrous. Company earnings had fallen back to 1982 levels, and we expected it to take two years to recover. Meanwhile, the stock was selling at a 38 percent premium to the market—significantly higher than we thought it was worth. Our recommendation: Sell, with a capital *S*.

A year and a half later, almost right on schedule, the company had recovered, its earnings had stablized. Baxter had streamlined operations by selling off five businesses. The company was also lowering its administrative and executive expenses. We expected the company to come on strong now, and its stock looked cheap. It sold at a market multiple, meaning Baxter's p/e ratio was the same as the Standard & Poor's index. It was well below the 38 percent premium to the market, where it was when we sold it. We bought it back again in size.

This was mid-August of 1987.

Well, we all remember what happened two months later. The stock market was annihilated in the Crash of '87. Everything took a beating. When the dust had settled a week and a half later, we looked around, surveyed the damage and issued this recommendation: "Baxter is down 9.3 percent since our August recommendation versus 25.8 percent for the S&P. A major victory! Sell it!"

How can a loss—any loss—be defined as a victory, much less a *major* victory?

First, if the story didn't pan out, you need to know when to cut your losses and move on. If you recognize your mistake before it becomes too compounded, then you're ahead of the game. You can make it up on a new idea. Second, if the market has gone down or other stocks in the same industry have gone south, then maybe your stock hasn't gone down as much. Relatively speaking, it's a winner. That was the case with Baxter. The stock had a lot further to fall than other stocks in its group, yet it kept some of its strength. At the same time, it has less room at the top to recover, so it's time to gather ourselves up and move on to a new idea

There is no magic formula for knowing when to cut and run. But there is a common mistake you'll want to avoid: Too often, when a stock has dropped, investors will tighten their grip on it, determined to make back that money. When the stock price rings in at their purchase price, they sell it. They consider it a moral victory. Well, I like moral victories as much as the next guy, but this is faulty reasoning on two fronts. First of all, suppose ABC Widget's stock price falls from $100 a share to $50 a share. It has dropped 50 percent. That means it has to improve *100 percent* to return to its original price. That's asking a lot of any stock. And heaven knows how long it could take.

The second point is a reminder: The market doesn't know or care where Mr. and Mrs. Investor bought their stock. It was up, it went down and it's come back up again. That doesn't mean the stock is done climbing. Maybe it's showing some strength. Maybe it's getting ready to make a big move. Too bad. Mr. and Mrs. Investor have bailed out at the wrong time with a moral victory. The common denominator in both points is lost time. The Investors could have spent that time working on new ideas that may have made more money faster, covering those earlier losses. As the old saying goes, time is as valuable a commodity as money.

THE END IS NEAR

Your hero in one period becomes the goat in the next. That's what happened with American Home Products and Abbott Laboratories. Both companies market a range of familiar consumer products as well as prescription drugs.

American Home Products is similar to Johnson & Johnson in the number of common household items and over-the-counter remedies it makes. Black Flag bug killer, Preparation H hemorrhoid treatment, Woolite detergent, Jiffy-Pop popcorn and Anacin are all part of the company's stable of products. Abbott includes Murine eye drops, Selsun shampoo and Similac infant formula. Obviously, these are companies that have wheedled their way into the everyday lives of a lot of people. That helps make them attractive investment targets. Nobody expects a mass migration away from such common, widely known and well-regarded products.

In Abbott's case, the company was virtually a rock. Its relative p/e valuation remained in the same tight range for over 20 years, making it easy to determine whether the stock was cheap or expensive. From the late 1960s, through the 1970s and into early 1980, I could always count on Abbott to sell at a premium to the market of 15 percent to 70 percent. In January of 1980, we looked ahead based on estimated earnings to see that Abbott's p/e ratio was at an 18 percent premium to the S&P 400, far into the low end of the company's range. This must be familiar to you now: If nothing is wrong with the company and stock looks cheap, buy it. So we did. The price was $38 a share. Shortly after that, the stock split 2-for-1. That gave us twice as much stock and, in effect, changed our original purchase price to $19 a share.

We traded Abbott very little during the next three years. The company was strong and stable and its stock remained a bargain until December 1982, when Abbott's p/e was 56 percent higher than the market's—the high end of the company's range. We sold the stock for $41 a share, up 116 percent from the $19 purchase price of 1980.

We traded in and out of Abbott the same way several times during the decade, each time picking up a few more dollars. The last time we sold it was April of 1992, when the stock rose 17 percent in eight months, four times faster than the market. The sell recommendation noted that Abbott "was among the best in the health care group, however, psychology in health care is atrocious." We needed to reduce our health and drug stock holdings.

If only I'd listened to myself.

American Home Products produced similar, though more modest, returns throughout the decade—rising 15 percent, 25 percent, 30 percent, even 33 percent in a few months each time we recommended it. But by the start of 1992, we were thrilled when it rose 7 percent in a flat market. Still, we recommended it again in February of 1992, followed five months later by the call, "abandon ship."

American Home Products was fine. There was nothing specifically wrong with the company or its products. It was the entire industry that was having its problems. The string had been played out, and we were taking too long to recognize it. In July of 1992, American Home Products was up a measly 2 percent in a market that had risen only half a point in that time. That was enough of a profit for us under the circumstances. Finally, it had sunk in: "A moral victory (there's that phrase again!) in a sloppy health care market."

While it had finally occurred to us that the fading days of health stocks had arrived, we were still about eight months late getting out of the group. At one point, as much as 18 percent of my portfolio was dedicated to heath care and pharmaceutical companies. Growth rates dropped from a frenetic 10 percent to 20 percent a year to a lackadaisical 0 percent to 12 percent. While I had a lot of success in that industry, the end was not my finest hour.

WHAT CHANGED?

Bill Clinton's victory in the 1992 presidential election started to take its toll on drug stocks even before the final ballot was cast. Clinton had made pharmaceutical companies the whipping boys for all the problems of health care, and he made it clear things would change under any health care plan he conceived.

In fact, Clinton's criticism was somewhat correct: The drug companies were gouging us and getting away with it through tremendous inflation in the cost of medicine over the decade. It was good for the drug companies, and it was good for me as an investor in drug companies. We made a lot of money.

You can see the power of the bully pulpit very clearly in the case of the drug companies. Clinton complained about health care and the cost of prescription drugs during his campaign. Early in his administration, he charged Hillary with fixing things. Within a year of his presidency, he had not passed a single law and had laid out a sketchy plan for health care reform, yet inflation in the industry had already dropped from about 8 percent a year to 2 percent. Competition is fierce for sick people and health maintenance organizations are becoming king.

The HMOs are the big buyers of drugs now, much more so than at the start of the '80s. Ten years ago, few people belonged to HMOs. Now, 25 percent of people are members. That's expected to rise quickly to 50 percent. Now, you aren't solely responsible for buying your medicine and billing your insurance company for it. The HMO takes control. Suppose you have three cholesterol drugs competing for all the clogged arteries of the world. One of those drug companies will probably be happy to offer its cholesterol medicine to a large HMO for a discount price—and an exclusive market. The market for drugs has been consolidated into powerful groups of doctors and administrators who can say what they'll pay for a drug—and get their price. Hospitals are also consolidating rapidly, exerting enormous pressure on drug and hospital supply pricing. It's bad news for both industries. So I'll move on, thank you very much. I wish I'd done it sooner.

15

The Feeling Is Mutual

After my morning's breakfast meeting with an analyst for a fellow stock trader, and before that first cup of coffee in the office, the first thing I do is dig through my copy of *The Wall Street Journal* for the stock listings. Am I looking for a hot stock that I heard about on the radio that morning? Nope. Nothing quite so exciting. Instead, buried with a million other names and numbers in tiny agate type, I can find my own portfolios listed. Printed in black and white, for all the world to see, is the price per share of my mutual funds and how they did compared with the day before. A quick calculation and I can tell how I did against the Standard & Poor's 500 index. Did my fund—the money I manage—rise or fall? By what percentage? And what did my bogey—the stock market itself—do that day?

As far as I'm concerned, those are pretty important numbers. It wouldn't be exaggerating too much to say that my job depends on them. And it wouldn't be surprising to find that a lot of folks all over the United States are looking at the same numbers every morning.

A lot of people depend on how well those numbers in *The Wall Street Journal* look. One of my jobs is to manage the SunTrust Corporate Equity Fund. My *real* job is to make money for the pension funds that invest their cash in my fund. Pension managers from cities, police and fire unions, small and large corporations have depended on my fund to make sure they can pay their retired employees a good pension. And while those people may not be too concerned with what happens from one day to the next, they are concerned about what happens from one quarter to the next or one year to the next.

I have said to them, "Give me your money; I'll invest it for you." Because they have neither the time nor perhaps the talent to invest the money successfully themselves, they have turned it over to me. They don't want it squandered. They want it to grow.

The same opportunity exists for individual investors. It's called the mutual fund. You've heard me mention them before in this book as an alternative to buying individual stocks and maintaining a large enough portfolio. But mutual funds are not an *alternative* to stocks as much as they are a way for the small (or large) investor to *reach* them. If I haven't made it clear already, let me try again: Investors should put their money in the stock market. That's where the biggest historical gains have been made throughout history—better than bonds, better than savings accounts, better than CDs, better than Treasury bills. History is on the stock market investor's side. *Everyone* should own stocks, somehow, some way. If you can't find a way to buy individual stocks, buy a mutual fund. Or, if you don't care to develop the expertise in stock picking, buy a mutual fund.

There is certainly no shame in that. I've done it myself. I have owned shares in the China Fund, a mutual fund that invests in Chinese companies, I know nothing about the companies that are based in China or that do business in China. I know nothing about China, but I do know this: I've been bullish on China. You've got 1.3 billion people and an economy growing faster than any other economy in the world. People there will make more money and buy motor scooters instead of bicycles, cars instead of scooters, home appliances, sewing machines. You've got a country poised to develop in the next 20 years the way the United States developed in the early twentieth century. So when the China Fund, a closed-end mutual fund that invests in Chinese companies, sold at a price below its net asset value, I bought it and let the fund manager make my decisions for me. They were good decisions; the fund did well. It doubled in a year! I couldn't have done that on my own.

Obviously, not everyone has $10,000 or $20,000 or $30,000 lying around waiting to be invested. Mutual funds are a great option, particularly if you can find one that matches your investment goals and seems to make money. Picking a mutual fund is not unlike starting your own individual investment portfolio. You need to have an investment style, you need to be willing to spend some money and you need to be able to stomach a few ups and downs from time to time.

That's what we'll talk about here.

WHAT'S A MUTUAL FUND?

The people who spend their money buying into a mutual fund are, in part, paying for the services of someone like me. They want someone who has a knack for choosing stocks or bonds, for making savvy investment decisions and for maximizing their money. Savvy investors in the stock market expect to lose money from time to time, but nobody invests in a mutual fund expecting to lose money. Mutual fund investors check the stock pages just as closely as stock market investors; if a mutual fund manager makes a mistake, then it shows up.

A mutual fund is a like a big club of small investors who pool their money into a massive pot and hire a professional investor to make that money grow. Each small investor buys shares in the mutual fund. As the fund grows (or shrinks) the profits (or losses) are divvied up based on each small investor's proportional share of the fund. Mutual funds have been established that cater to just about every style of investor. Some mutuals funds hope to reap large gains by investing in small, newly emerging growth companies, although the risk is higher. Others invest in money market accounts, reaping smaller and steadier returns—without the chance of a gain or loss in principal. One key to remember: Investors who buy shares in a mutual fund that invests in the stock market *do not* own stock in any of those companies; they only own shares of the fund. Our company runs the STI Classic family of funds. STI is the stock symbol for SunTrust Banks. My fund is the Capital Growth Fund.

Fortunately, I didn't know about mutual funds when I first started investing in the early 1960s. If I had, I might have put my meager savings to work there instead of spending $280 to buy 10 shares of United Fruit. I might not have found my talent for stock picking and might not be where I am today—and I'm very happy where I am today. At the time I invested in United Fruit, mutual funds were small potatoes. Although they had been around for at least three decades at that point, they were not big business, the way they have become today. They did not become really big until the 1980s.

At that time, when the bulls were running wild on Wall Street and the stock market could seemingly do no wrong, mutual funds began to become a major feature on the investment terrain. They were the tool small investors could use to buy stock diversity without spending too much money or too much time. People who didn't have large sums to spend on stocks found they could catch some of the market mania by buying mutual funds. They also noticed (wisely) that their financial returns from savings accounts, certificates of deposit or money market accounts paled in comparison to the returns they could reap from mutual funds.

Mutual funds come in two major varieties: *Closed-end* and *open-end*. The latter, in turn, can be divided into *no-load* and *load* funds. Investment books and money guides that were apparently written by MBAs from Harvard spend an awful lot of words to explain these concepts. We'll stick to the English language here, and you'll see that they are very simple.

Closed-end funds offer a limited number of shares that can be traded on the open market, just as a company's stock is traded. For example, the ABC Fund might only offer a million shares in the fund. Once those million shares are sold, no one else can buy into the fund unless existing shareholders sell some of their shares. Shareholders would offer their shares on the open market, and the shares would sell for whatever price is available—again, just like shares of stock in a company.

Open-end mutual funds offer shares to anyone who wants to buy. The fund will sell as many shares to as many people who want them. The shares of open-end mutual funds are not traded on an exchange. That gives holders the advantage of making them very easy to sell; shareholders simply sell shares back to the fund. The price of those shares is simply the "net asset value" (NAV) of the fund: How much are the fund's holdings worth, divided by the number of outstanding shares. Where closed-end funds can trade for more (or less) than their net asset value, based on how popular they appear to be in the open market, an open-end fund trades at its NAV. Suppose today the XYZ Fund has 10 shares outstanding and $200 worth of assets. XYZ's net asset value is $20. I sell a share back to the fund, which then pays me the $20. Now, there are nine shares outstanding; the value of XYZ's assets is now $180, so the net asset value is still $20—until trading opens tomorrow and the fund manager starts buying and selling stocks again.

Load and no-load are even easier expressions to explain. A mutual fund that includes a load usually charges a commission for the purchase of its shares—sometimes as much as 8.5 percent of the price. That's too high. I don't recommend paying more than 3.5 percent for a fund's load; any more is just too much to pay the salesman.

A no-load fund does not charge a commission. Both kinds of funds, however, would charge a *management fee* in the neighborhood of 1 percent, to cover such things as the fund manager's salary, analysts and other costs (as well as the fund's profit). Studies have shown that there is no difference in performance between load and no-load funds. And there is absolutely no reason why their performance should be different.

Mutual funds have become so popular, there are more of them on the market than actual stocks. By the end of 1993, the Investment Company Institute, a Washington, D.C.–based trade group, estimated there were at least 4,500 mutual funds holding nearly $2 *trillion* in assets. Those funds are grouped and managed in a variety of forms for practically any investment appetite. If you're hungry for a chance to reap the gains of the stock market, but not willing to accept too much of its risk, then you can buy funds that build their portfolio's holdings to reflect a stock market index such as the Standard & Poor's 500, so the fund would do exactly as well as the market as a whole. You can buy funds that invest exclusively in foreign stocks, and you can buy funds that invest only in bonds. You can even buy mutual funds that invest in a variety of *other* mutual funds.

So What's the Big Deal?

If Kinder-Care had been my first experience in the stock market, I might have found myself slaving over one of those hateful computers in the actuarial department for some insurance company today. Novice investors who try their hand at the stock market can't expect success from the get-go if they buy one stock, or two stocks and expect to make a killing. That happens only to the lucky or the criminal. I was lucky.

So that's the big deal about mutual funds. They offer *diversity*. And the good ones offer top-flight fund management.

In the stock market, you can't expect to be diversified unless you're willing to spend $30,000 to $100,000 so you can buy a variety of stocks in different industries. More than that would be better. Once you get up to 25 stocks in your portfolio, you're quite well diversified. You can expect to see some stocks fall and many stocks rise if you're smart about your investments.

However, that's a lot of money in anybody's book. For a tenth of that, you can often open a mutual fund account by calling the fund directly or by consulting with a stockbroker. I recommend it to small investors or even to large investors who don't care to take the time to study the market, watch individual stocks and pay close attention to a portfolio. That doesn't mean mutual fund investors are completely off the hook; their workload may not be as heavy, but they still need to pay attention. I said before, an investor who isn't paying attention to his investments is destined to lose them.

DOS AND DON'TS

What's your mutual fund style? Buying individual stocks and building a portfolio from scratch is somewhat akin to buying a custom-made suit. You decide what style you're going for, whether it's flashy or conservative. You buy the latest fashion magazines to see what suits are in and what styles are out. You consult with a tailor to get the right material, make the measurements and create the right fit. When you're building that portfolio, you're consulting investment magazines and journals, reading *Value Line*, talking to your stock-broker and working out your investment "style." You're trying to get the right fit.

Buying a mutual fund is no different from buying that suit off the rack. You still want it to conform to your own style, whether it's flashy or conservative, growth stocks or bonds. And you still want it to fit correctly. You're just not inclined to spend the time or the money to have it custom tailored.

When you go shopping for a mutual fund, you need to establish your investment goals and your investment style just as clearly as you would if you were buying individual stocks. In the world of mutual funds, there are funds to accommodate just about any style.

Are you interested in very little risk and regular income? That may be your style if you're an older investor who doesn't have a lot of time to wait for an investment to build. In that case, you might be interested in a fund that invests in municipal bonds or money markets or slow-growth, high-dividend paying stocks such as utilities.

Perhaps you want the chance to reap large growth in the fund, although it may require a little more risk. You're the one who would be buying stock in small but fast-growing companies (like The

Home Depot in the mid-1980s) if you had the money; instead, you can buy mutual funds that focus on those kinds of companies. That may be for the younger investors who are saving for a child's education or their own retirement.

Maybe you could handle a little more risk and buy into a fund that invests in very, very new companies, those that don't even have their products on the market yet.

Before you slip on that suit jacket, you'll want to browse the aisles of the investment magazines such as *Fortune, Forbes* and *Money* (and others), which include annual reports on hundreds of different funds—including their performance record for the past year, 5 years and 10 years. That obviously won't tell you what the fund will do in the next year (or 5), but it will tell you how consistently it has performed in the past. You want a fund that has done well relative to its bogey. If the fund invests in large growth companies, how has it done next to a stock market index of large-company growth stocks? You'll also want to get a copy of the fund's annual report, which outlines its investment strategy, its goals and the specific investments it makes. In fact, you should expect to receive a copy of the prospectus before you buy shares in a mutual fund.

Just as you shouldn't change your investment style from quarter to quarter when you buy individual stocks, you shouldn't change mutual funds from year to year and expect to see growth. If the fund is not performing, obviously you might want to consider another one. But one style of investing will not fit every economic cycle. Trying to time your investment style to fit a particular cycle won't work any better with mutual funds than it will with individual stocks. If your fund is struggling during a particular cycle because its style is out of favor, maybe that is the time to buy more.

Diversify: You thought you were diverse enough by buying a mutual fund, right? Wrong. If you buy one mutual fund, you're putting your nest egg in the hands of one money manager with one investment style. Sure, that's what you'd be doing if you ran your own stock portfolio, but why limit yourself when you can choose mutual funds with a variety of styles, expectations and strategies?

There are stock funds, bond funds, foreign stock funds, value funds—why not own two or three different funds? That protects you and your money twice: First, when the economy favors a particular style of investing (say, small growth stocks) you benefit from the hot market. But when the economy doesn't favor that style, you've got money in other funds to help bolster your holdings. Second, a portfolio manager gets a hot hand sometimes; everything the hand touches turns to gold. Other times, it gets cold. If you wisely spread your money around to a variety of funds, you have a better chance of catching a manager on a hot streak. You won't hit a home run investing this way, but you should get a lot of singles and doubles.

Stocks! Do I have to say it again? If you really expect to make any money and see substantial growth in your investments, buy shares in mutual funds that invest in the stock market. I just mentioned some ideas for funds that invest in other areas (such as money markets). Those aren't my idea of investments any more than a certificate of deposit is an investment.

Don't limit yourself: Some mutual funds bend over backward to accommodate the philosophy and ethics of their investors. Some funds forbid the purchase of "sin" stocks such as tobacco or alcohol companies. In the 1980s, before the reforms in South Africa, some funds would forbid the purchase of stock in companies that did business in that country. Some funds focus on particular sectors of the economy; a fund might only invest in "environmental services," for example, such as solid waste disposal companies or recycling companies.

I suppose that's good for the conscience of some investors, but only if they don't expect to make a lot of money. Those are "socially acceptable," but you're investing to make money, not to make a social statement. If you want to make a social statement, give to the United Way or your church. Why limit yourself? Why put your money into a fund that ties the hands of its money managers? When the economic cycle for "environmental service" companies is bad, how can the fund do anything to counteract that trend?

Fact is, you could drive yourself batty trying to make all your investments socially as well as fiscally sound. If you carried lofty social goals to their extreme, then maybe a good Catholic investor wouldn't have some health care stocks in the 1980s because many of those companies made money on birth control pills. Maybe others would avoid stock in Sara Lee because they object to the level of cholesterol in their pastries (even though pastry is a small portion of Sara Lee's business). Some might avoid defense stocks.

Remember why you're investing in the first place.

As a money manager, I divide my stock holdings into different categories by industry. I can closely monitor which industries are doing well, buying or selling in or out of them as they fall in or out of favor. My hands aren't tied; why should yours be?

Wait: Don't buy into the initial offering of a closed-end mutual fund. That's a good way to throw away some of your money's buying power. Remember: A closed-end mutual fund sells only a limited number of shares. Once those shares are gone, nobody can buy into the fund until an existing shareholder decides to sell some off. Now suppose the initial offering price is $20 a share. I'd estimate that about a dollar of that goes to pay the underwriter who is doing all the paperwork involved in the initial offering of this mutual fund. That leaves only 19 of your dollars for the fund manager to invest. You've given away the first 5 percent.

Gains and losses: Don't buy mutual funds that have large unrealized gains in them—unless you happen to like the IRS.

Huh?

I hope this is as close to corporate-speak as I get in this book. But the concept is important. Let's break it down and muddle through. Let's suppose you own stock in ABC Widget (again). If you bought ABC stock at $10 a share and it rose to $30 a share, but you haven't sold the stock, you'd have an unrealized gain of $20. You "realize" that gain the moment you sell it. You also have to pay income taxes on that "realized gain."

Now suppose you're the manager of a mutual fund and you own shares in a lot of companies that did well. The share price has gone up on all of them—but you haven't sold any of the stock. That's the unrealized gain. When you sell those shares, your mutual fund realizes all those gains and the profits money is spread around to the mutual fund's shareholders—all of whom must pay taxes on those gains. But the fact is, you weren't around to make the gain. You bought in and surprise! There's a bunch of money that you must pay tax on.

You can tell if a fund has unrealized gains by reading the fund's annual report and comparing the value of the fund's holdings against its costs. The funds I manage have a high turnover; I buy and sell stocks actively, so my asset value and my cost is relatively close. In other words, I don't let stocks sit around very long with unrealized gains. I want the money in my hands, working for me on another stock idea.

If you have a lot of money in the market, it pays to follow things closely; if you want to have a lot of money in the market, but you don't have the time to follow things *that* closely, you need to let someone else do it for you.

That is what mutual funds are for.

A Little Q & A about Mutual Funds

What's the best fund for me?

Before you buy a mutual fund, ask yourself these questions: What is my objective? What am I hoping to accomplish? If you don't know what you want, how will you get it? Do you want stocks, bonds, real estate, and so forth? If it's bonds, do you want tax-free income? Taxable? High income? Low volatility? High- or low-quality bonds? (High quality means lower returns but less risk; low quality means possibly higher returns and probably higher risk.)

In other words, match up your objectives and needs and risk level with that of the fund's. If you already have a good growth fund, consider one with different traits. Again: diversify. There is no reason to hold five different growth funds.

WHAT IS THE RECORD OF THE FUND?

A one year record is not sufficient. Try 5- and 10-year records. How did it do against funds with the same objective? What is the size of that fund versus the size when the record was the best? I've said it before: It's a lot harder to run a $5 billion fund successfully than a $500 million fund. Is the fund manager the same as it was when this record was compiled?

WHAT DOES IT COST?

Check the sales fees. I don't recommend paying a front-end load (the cost of buying *in* to the fund) of more than 3.5 percent. If you have to pay to get *out* of the fund too, I recommend that the combined front-end and rear-end load should not exceed 4 percent. Management fees and incidental fees should not exceed 1.1 percent a year.

16

What the Future Holds

Early on, we spent a chapter discussing a day in my life as an institutional investor, following the sort of conversations and phone calls I get, so I could give you a glimpse at what my investment style is like. During that particular day, I happened to have quite a bit of cash on hand, and I was looking for some good companies to buy cheaply. One in particular I was on the prowl for: Hillenbrand Industries. I wanted very much to find 200,000 shares of this Indiana company that showed solid earnings growth—sometimes more than 20 percent a year—during the last half of the 1980s and the early 1990s. At the time of this writing, it is a fantastic company.

Still majority-owned by the Hillenbrand family, the company's stock did nothing but climb during the late '80s and early '90s. Earnings grew more than 15 percent a year since 1979. That's a record I find admirable in any company—good, consistent growth. Obviously, good management had a lot to do with that record. But there may be another good reason for it.

This company is the world leader in building caskets.

In fact, Hillenbrand Industries makes most of its money building something else nobody wants to lie in: hospital beds. Slightly more than half its revenues come from making hospital beds and other assorted home-care medical supplies. Nearly all of the other half comes from selling caskets to more than 16,000 funeral directors in the United States and Canada and selling funeral insurance and planning services to 4,000 funeral directors. (Hillenbrand also made American Tourister luggage; the company agreed to sell its luggage division in August 1993.) The company has bought out other casket makers, including the 1992 purchase of a large Canadian casket company.

So, you might ask, what does this mean? Why is a casket company a good bet for the future, and why do I want to own stock in it? It's a fair question. The best reason, of course, is that this is an excellent company that would probably do well in any business. The fact is, they're in the casket and hospital bed business. Their products are better and cheaper than those of the competition. And, at the risk of being morbid, I'll put it bluntly: the baby-boom generation is getting old. Who is the ultimate beneficiary of an aging population?

Let me digress for a moment: I said earlier that you are the one who must make investment decisions for yourself. I also said you need to read and listen to as much information as you can find. So while you don't want demographers and economists to make investment decisions for you (heaven forbid!), you've got to listen to what they're saying from time to time. And what they're saying lately isn't good news for me. It might be good news for you, depending on the investment style you adopt, but I have lower expectations for my investment future than I did in the 1980s, when the look of America was different than it is expected to be in the 1990s and beyond. I'll elaborate on that later.

The demographers have filled the media with an alphabet soup of acronyms that are amusing to hear until you start to realize what they mean for investors. Yuppies, we know already as "young urban professionals." Do you know what VUMMIES, DINKS, OINKS, NIKES and SITCOMS are? They translate as "very upwardly mobile mommies"; "dual income, no kids"; "one income, no kids"; the very frightening "no income kids with education" and the terrifying "single income, two children, outrageous mortgage." These silly syllables describe trends in our population that demographers expect through the year 2000 and into the next millennium.

Through this chapter, we will begin to see why all this means a casket company could be good investment news for everyone but the person who is lying in one.

Changing Times

I have always paid cash for my autos. Even when I took home only $376 a month in my first job in the early 1960s, I didn't take out a car loan—not even for my first car. It was a Chrysler Valiant convertible, for my money one of the two best cars ever made for a long time. Give me a Valiant or a Dodge Dart anytime. They were great cars. I paid $2,700 for the Valiant, although I didn't really save the money for that car. I've been saving money all my life. I wasn't saving for a car; I was just *saving* as usual.

I continued saving and investing throughout the 1960s and into the 1970s, when I worked for the U.S. Public Health Service and for Lincoln National Life and in assorted other jobs that have faded into obscurity. By 1979, after the stock market had basically curled up and died for 11 years, a friend whom I hadn't seen for 16 years asked me if I still bought stocks for myself. I told him all my money was in stocks. He couldn't understand it. He said he didn't know anyone who was invested in the stock market at the time. Ten years later, people were throwing their money at the stock market and mutual funds with reckless abandon. It wasn't hard to see why they were reluctant at the time, but the masses were wrong.

The United States had massive inflation during the '70s and early '80s, and the stock market couldn't keep up with it. We had two oil crises, a ballooning national debt and double-digit inflation and interest rates. We were in the midst of the "malaise." All this culminated with the election of Ronald Reagan. By the time the bulls started the stir on Wall Street, around 1982, investors were ready for something to happen—*anything*.

Twenty years after I bought that Valiant, times had changed a lot. For one thing, I didn't have the Valiant anymore. For another, the Reagan years were in full swing. The oil crisis had ended. Corporations started to change and streamline, earnings picked up, inflation dropped. Everything was working. While I continued saving and investing my money, most of America didn't. Massive tax cuts had put money in people's pockets. Consumer confidence started to brim over. The savings rate in the United States dropped from about 8.5 percent at the start of the 1980s to less than 4 percent by the end.

If consumers aren't saving their money, that means they're spending it. And spend it they did! In economic terms, the 1980s are renowned for nothing if not corporate greed and consumer debt. Conspicuous consumption was the way of the world at the time as Yuppies plunked down their paychecks to buy BMWs, houses and designer clothes. They wanted VCRs and televisions with remote controls, Reebok sneakers for $100 a pair, videotape cameras, personal computers, washers and dryers.

And they wanted them *now*.

It meant consumer stocks were king. Packaged food companies flourished (as we discussed earlier) as these new consumers started setting up households. Retailers had the time of their life. This is the period when Wal-Mart started to break out of the small-town markets and into the urban areas. Japan's economy couldn't have fared better, thanks to its virtual monopoly on many of the consumer items that young consumers wanted at the time, particularly electronic toys such as VCRs, video games, televisions, Toyotas and Hondas. Times may be tougher for Japan's consumer-based economy in the coming years.

WHAT WAS HAPPENING?

Here comes that word again: demographics.

For the U.S. economy, the demographics couldn't have been more favorable. To put it simply, the biggest chunk of the postwar baby boomers had finally grown up. In 1986, the United States had

more 25-year-olds than ever before—about 4.5 million of them—
and obviously many millions more citizens in the 20- to 40-year-
old range.

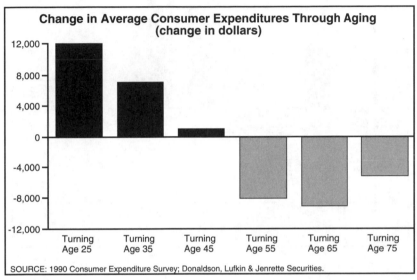

Fig. 16-1

These are the people who do the buying (see Figure 16-1).
They're the ones striking out from college for the first time, finding apartments and houses, buying cars, going to the movies, ac-
quiring new appliances, building families and getting married (with
all those attendant expenses). It is the prime consuming age. The
U.S. economy was flush with buyers, consumers and spenders. We
entered the longest period of nonstop economic growth in history.

Of course, that couldn't last forever.

As with everything, demographics change. You'll see in the next
graph (Figure 16-2) that the group of folks aged 40 to 60 years old
grow the fastest before the turn of the century. The baby boomers,
once the driving force for economic boom time, get to be another
10 or 20 years older. And as they creep up on age 45, they stop being
big spenders. They've bought all the houses, cars and clothes they
need—maybe that's why they're so hard to buy for when Christmas rolls around. You can't think of anything they need!

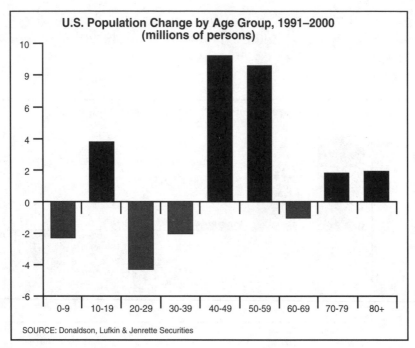

Fig. 16-2

Even worse, as they get older still, they'll become more of a strain on the economy, on the Social Security system, on the health care system. And the U.S. Census Bureau tells us that elderly folks are going to command a lot more attention in a few years. In 1993, Americans over age 65 make up about one out of every eight of us. By 2050, one out of every five of us will be over 65. Baby boomers will drop from a third of the population in 1993 to a fourth of the population by 2010. We're getting older.

And these aren't *projections.* These are facts. We know how many 20-year-olds there are today, so we have a pretty good idea how many 30-year-olds there will be in 10 years, right? That's one reason we can look at that chart and figure on a slight upturn in the number of 25-year-olds until 1996 (good news for the consumer economy), but those numbers will start sliding back down after that (more bad news).

The demographers sketch a few other trends onto the canvas of what we know about the "aging of America" to create a portrait that is spelled out in those acronyms at the beginning of the chapter.

VUMMIES: Very upwardly mobile mommies are the women who are are marrying later (if at all) in the years leading up to the next century. Divorce is still a growing fact of life. More women are working and making households for themselves.

DINKS: There will also be a lot of "dual-income, no kids" households. Baby boomers are becoming the first generation of Americans to have more siblings than children.

OINKS: Folks with "one income, no kids" are waiting longer to marry and have children.

NIKES: Ouch! These are a parent's worst nightmare. The "no income kids with education" finished college and *moved back home*. Experts say it's been happening already. For example, the percentage of 25-year-old men who moved back home rose from just over 10 percent in 1980 to about 15 percent in 1992. (For women, the stats are less chilling: about 8.5 percent in 1980, about 10 percent in 1992.) The problem with NIKES is simple: It reduces the bonus of having 25-year-olds in the economy. Instead of being ravenous consumers, they're dependents again.

SITCOMS: See VUMMIES, and remember Yuppies? Then factor in the shortage of housing that economists expect to show up as baby boomers continue to swamp the housing market. This translates into "single income, two children, outrageous mortgage." People paying off debts aren't putting more money into the economy. They're not consuming. They're just digging out of a hole.

AND GOVERNMENTS CHANGE

All this demographic mumbo jumbo wasn't happening in a vacuum, of course. Presidents Reagan and Bush, with their pro–Big Business, anti–Big Government attitude, came and left. The wild economic growth couldn't sustain itself forever. And President Clinton, with a different attitude, had come into the White House.

Now you have a different agenda from Washington, D.C., laid across the demographic changes we're seeing. Instead of Big Business and power to the private sector, we're seeing more of a "share the wealth" mentality. Clinton believes there is a finite amount of wealth in this country and that it must be spread around to as many people as possible. If someone is rich, then that means someone else must be poor. I certainly don't agree. I have always felt there is un-limited wealth—it's just a matter of finding it and building it.

As I write this, I note that Clinton has so far been decidedly pro-government, anti–Big Business and anti-rich people. He has tended to dislike the very things that made the 1980s an excellent decade for investors. I expect taxes aimed at the wealthy individu-als and the wealthy corporations to further dampen consumer sen-timent and consumer spending. All this works against the stock market. For investors, there will be a completely different set of priorities. It means a lot of industries that did well in the 1980s will do poorly in the 1990s—health care stocks are a prime example, as we discussed earlier.

I can almost guarantee that the years leading up through the turn of the century won't be as good as the 1980s. Some will say that depends on who you are.

WHERE TO INVEST?

I bought heavily into the banking industry in 1990, then sold out almost completely by 1991. I bought back in heavily in 1992 and had sold half my holdings by the end of 1993. Retailing looked awful. Where once you could expect 10 percent or 30 percent growth, growth had become flat. Once upon a time, a chain could open a new store and find a way to boost revenues without hurting competitors; suddenly a new store had to take business from an-other store to stay afloat. I hadn't found many stocks or industries that excited me by the time I started writing this book. I hadn't found many more by the time I had finished it either. I even gave more attention to technology stocks—but I kept a long list of them handy to swap in and out, because I don't trust any of them.

In short, I had been floundering around, trying to figure out the best way to play the aging of America.

Many of the stocks I liked in the 1980s are not the place to be in the environment we expect in the 1990s and beyond. In my boom years, I had large chunks of money in packaged food, health care, and retailing. I had very little money in industries such as energy and public utilities. You couldn't have asked for a smarter decision at the time, and there were a lot of investors who weren't making those kinds of decisions. They had money in energy and not in packaged foods. Those people probably don't have their jobs anymore.

And I hate energy stocks. If they didn't make up such a large portion of the market (as much as 12 percent), I probably wouldn't waste my time with them at all. Here's an industry that mixes a deadly brew: Companies in this industry obviously deal with a commodity (which is, by its nature, volatile and unpredictable) and they are dependent on politics (which is also volatile and unpredictable). Two strikes are plenty for me.

Now, all the stocks I hate may be the ones that will probably do well: energy companies, paper companies, auto companies, chemical stocks. These are generally cyclical stocks that improve (or weaken) as the economy gets better (or worse). A paper company that might not have seen much growth in demand for its products during a weak economy could see improved sales as the outlook gets brighter and clients can afford to start spending again. I don't like these companies long term, but I can't ignore them when they have their moment to shine. The trouble is knowing when that shine is coming.

The tables may have turned on me a little bit, but that's okay. It will probably be more of a struggle for me to outperform the market (that's always been my one and only goal), but *I still expect to outperform the market.* Markets change, but you can't change your investment style. I'm not inclined to change the way I do business. That's a sure recipe for failure. I'm still going to look for growth and try to buy it cheap. And almost anything that's cheap enough will catch my interest. I'll still buy stocks at a discount to where I think they should sell and wait until the perception catches up with the reality. When they're priced at a premium, I'll sell them again and look for the next bargain.

While I'm more subdued about the stock market these days, that doesn't mean I think you shouldn't be invested in the stock market. If the market grows at a more modest rate of 6 percent to 7 percent a year with a 2 percent or 3 percent dividend yield, that's way off from the boom time we've experienced in the recent past. But it's still enviable next to the meager 3 percent you can expect from your money markets and your certificates of deposit. I'm a believer in the stock market as a winner in any economic period.

And maybe, as I settle my pre-baby-boomer body into an easy chair, the casket companies will take off.

INSIDE LINE

In 1920, a 30-year-old immigrant in the United States, named Charles Ponzi, offered investors the chance to make 50 percent on their money in just six weeks. It became the classic investment scam of the industry: the Ponzi Scheme. The idea: You pony up a certain amount of money up front and recruit others behind you to pony up too. The investors who come in later supply the capital that provides enormous profits for those who came in early. But eventually, the whole system collapses when there are too many people in the pyramid and not enough cash to pay them back.

Not even three decades after Ponzi escaped with $10 million, Franklin Roosevelt created a Ponzi scheme on the United States that could collapse any time now, thanks to the demographics we just discussed. He called it Social Security.

In the '90s, we have about five workers in the U.S. labor pool for every retiree who is benefitting from a Social Security payment. In a few years, as the Census Bureau and the economists are telling us, that's likely to go down to three workers for every retired Social Security recipient. See how this works? As time goes on, the base of the Ponzi "pyramid" grows smaller and smaller. More and more people rise to the top, expecting to get their Social Security checks after they turn 65. But a smaller and smaller proportion of people are paying into the system.

What's going to happen?

Who knows? But we do know this: The American Association of Retired Persons is the largest lobbying group in Washington already. Today's workers are probably going to be working a lot harder for someone else's future, or they're going to be working a lot longer for their own. As one politician said: "Of course you'll get your pension. It just might not be worth anything once you get it."

17

Dos and Don'ts

When the idea of writing an investment book first rolled around, I was a little skeptical. I had read some of them and frankly, didn't learn much I didn't already know. Sometimes, in fact, I learned things I didn't really want to know. Nobody's get-rich-quick scheme or invest-without-risk idea offered much for the average investor. Investing is something you must learn by doing. I've tried to make that point throughout this book. You can't read my words and copy my technique and expect to make a bundle. Even if you could copy my investment style, what would happen if there were 1,000 Tony Grays stomping around on Wall Street? Chilling thought, when you think about all those bargain-basement suits and Nebraska accents. But do you think they'd all be successful?

No, there are no magic formulas for stock market success. But now that I'm well into this book, that won't stop me from sharing more of my advice. These dos and don'ts—some of them mentioned earlier in the book—reflect the philosophy of an investor who likes doing things the old-fashioned way: Buy cheap, sell expensive. Buy stocks. Don't play tricks or use fancy footwork. There's plenty of money to be made in the stock market without resorting to high-finance games. Leave that for the Wall Street MBAs who think they have the whole thing figured out, but actually don't do any better than you and I could do with simple hard work and good sense.

TRICKS OF TRADING

Now that I've mentioned them, you'll want to know what I'm talking about. And it's probably a good idea to understand a little bit about these fancy, stock market trading ideas. You'll want to understand enough to know that you don't want to try them. I know I don't. Maybe I'm lazy. Maybe I just don't want to learn something new. Or maybe I'm just content with the success I've had doing things the way I've always done them. You decide. By the way: None of these examples factor in the cost of commissions and fees, which can be considerable. For the sake of simplicity, we're assuming that your broker is working for free.

Don't buy on margin. You say you don't have enough money to dive headfirst into the stock market? No problem, the experts would have you believe. Buying on margin will let you pump up your investment capital—even double it if that's what you want to do. Here's how it works: Suppose you want to invest $1,000 in the stock market. You borrow $500 from your broker and toss in $500 yourself. Then buy stock. Let's make it easy and say you buy 1,000 shares of ABC Widget at $1 each. If the stock goes up 50 percent, to $1.50 a share, you sell your stock for a total of $1,500. From that money, you must repay the $500 you borrowed from your broker. That leaves $1,000. You started with $500 of your own money and ended up with $1,000—you doubled your money!

Sounds pretty good, doesn't it?

In fact, you're borrowing money to bet on the horse races. It's the same as walking into a track with borrowed money. You've got a guy with a bad attitude breathing down your neck, the next day, waiting to get paid after your horse comes in. Of course, he expects to get paid even if your horse *doesn't* come in. So does your broker.

Let's look at our example again.

However, this time, let's assume ABC Widget's stock gets some bad news: It drops in half, to $.50 a share. Now, you've paid $1,000 for a stock that's only worth $500. You could pay back your broker if you sold the stock now, and you'd be out $500 of your own money. You've just lost *all* your money. Meanwhile, your broker would have already made a "margin call," insisting that you bring in more cash to cover your debt if the stock continued to fall. Heinous crimes have been committed over margin calls by investors who didn't have the money.

I don't recommend buying on margin.

Don't sell stocks short. This is the opposite of logic, the opposite of the Wall Street proverb about buying low and selling high. Short sellers reverse the order: "Sell high, buy low." They're betting on the price of a stock to fall. It's almost anti-American, isn't it? The short-seller's success depends on calamity striking a corporation. Here's how it works:

Instead of borrowing cash from a broker, you actually borrow stock. Let's use those 1,000 shares of ABC Widget as an example. You borrow the stock and sell it for $1 a share, receiving a tidy $1,000. Then, you wait. You're waiting for the bad news to hit ABC, for its earnings to drop, for a recession to hit, for a massive accident at ABC's biggest plant, for another short seller to start an unfounded rumor about the company—anything that will make the price of ABC stock fall. Then, it happens.

The price drops to $.50 a share. You buy back 1,000 shares of ABC stock, but you only have to spend $500 out of that $1,000 pool to do it. You return the 1,000 shares of stock to your broker and keep $500 for yourself. Again, it sounds pretty simple, right?

I don't recommend this technique for two reasons. First, I just don't think it's a good bet. You're betting on the stock price to fall, right? Well, over the years, the stock market has shown an upward bias. The market *wants* to rise. Prices want to increase. If you believe that to be the case, why would you bet on a stock to fall?

Second, just look at the simple math: If you buy a stock and it falls, the worst it can do is drop to nothing. You buy ABC Widget for $1,000 and it goes out of business the next day. You've lost $1,000. It can't go down any more than that. But suppose you short ABC's stock. You hope the price falls because if it rises, you'll have to spend more money to buy back the stock and return it to your broker. The higher it goes, the more you must spend to replace those borrowed shares. And while a stock price can *fall* a definite, measurable amount (to zero), it can *rise* forever. Suppose ABC Widget gets a lucrative government contract, wins a favorable ruling in an antitrust lawsuit and patents a revolutionary new widget design all in the same day. Suddenly, you might have to pay $2,000 or $3,000 to buy back those 1,000 shares of stock. And that's just a start. It's a long way to infinity. Someone probably shorted Wal-Mart in the 1970s on its way from $.50 a share to $30.00. I don't have any sympathy for him.

Don't buy options. This is truly a testament to my laziness. I don't want to do options because, frankly, they're complicated, time consuming to manage, their commissions are very high and they aren't very easy to buy or sell. I don't recommend them. Like any other investment, this technique is a bet on stocks. In this case, you're laying down a certain amount of money, betting that a stock will rise (or fall) to a certain price within a certain amount of time. Within that period, you have the right to buy (or sell) the stock, depending on what kind of option you've bought. Again, this is a very complicated form of investing. It's a way of buying and selling the *chance* to buy stock, without spending the kind of money it costs to buy the actual stock. Any explanation I give of options is going to be oversimplified, but let's give it a whirl anyway.

Options are usually bought and sold as though they were stocks and bonds, although an option is exactly that—just an *option* to buy or sell a stock at a certain price within a certain amount of time. Most options buyers don't ever exercise the option; they simply trade it to someone else.

What does an option represent? Suppose you pay someone $2 for the *option* to buy ABC Widget's stock at $20 a share within three months. If the stock is selling at $18, you're betting that it will rise at least $4 a share within three months. You're "locking in" the chance to buy the stock cheaper if it goes up a lot. If ABC rises to $22 in a few weeks, you *could* exercise your option—buy shares in ABC at $20 each, then turn around and sell them at the market price. You'll make nothing. More likely, you won't shell out the money for the stock. You'll just sell the option for a few dollars per share more than you paid, giving someone else the option to "lock in" that $20 price.

But if the price of ABC Widget remains $18 a share, you don't have to exercise your option; you lose the $2 premium you paid at the outset. Remember: You never owned a single share of ABC. You just owned the *chance* to own the stock.

The same applies if you pay for a "sell" option. You don't own any shares of ABC Widget, but you are paying for the option to sell those shares anyway. Suppose you pay someone $2 for the option to *sell* ABC Widget's stock at $20 a share within three months. If the stock now sells at $20 a share, you're paying $2 to insure that you still have the chance to sell that stock for $20 three months later—even if it falls to $18 on the open market. If it does fall below $20, you *could* exercise your option. You'd buy the stock in the open market at $18, then exercise your option by selling it for the agreed-upon $20 a share, making $2 a share in the process. More than likely, however, you'd *sell* your option, which is worth a little more than you paid for it, to someone else. That person would pay you for the chance to lock in the $20-per-share selling price. The trading price rises or falls depending on what kind of option it is and how much time remains before the option expires.

If this sounds complicated, there's a good reason for it. Options *are* complicated. Avoid them. The vast majority of investors who buy and sell options lose money. 'Nuff said!

SLINKYS AND CABBAGE PATCHES

Anyone remember Cabbage Patch Kids? The Toy of the Century a few years ago, the ugly little doll that every child had to own, is now relegated to a small shelf in the toy store somewhere. How about Pong? It was the rage in video-game technology for a few years, until Pac-Man and his sisters and brothers made the old blip-blip of electronic tennis obsolete. Today's video games make Pac-Man look prehistoric by comparison. These are the fads of the toy industry, the products that earn a quick buck for their inventor and move quickly into obscurity. These are not the Slinkys of the world, the age-old, enduring toys that have made such a mark in society that they are now sold as desktop ornaments for button-down executives.

If you can, do resist the urge to let fads influence your investment decisions. My best example: high tech. If I never had to invest in another technology stock, it would be too soon for my liking. I am weary of watching Intel invent a new computer chip, spending millions to develop it, then spending millions more to stop Advanced Micro Devices or some other high-tech company from copying it. One reason I'm weary of it: That chip will be old news in a few years anyway. Someone, somewhere will come along with a faster, more powerful computer chip. And it won't take long.

To me, the whole high-tech industry is one big fad after another. One company gets a minor lead against another one, then another steals it back with a "major" breakthrough. In high tech, it's easy for a company that invents the newest, neatest black box to leap from nowhere to somewhere, but the shelf life is so short, there's no time to make money on it.

Meanwhile, profitability in the personal computer industry is in shambles; prices are falling. It has none of the characteristics of an industry you ought to like. I invest in technology only when I have to, and mostly because my portfolio is so large that I can't afford to ignore it. Like it or not, high tech affects the stock market.

My only hope: Invest in the companies that *support* the high-tech industry. From time to time, I have put my money in companies that create computer networks and write software so computers can talk to each other, companies such as Novell, Cisco or EDS (Ross Perot's old company). And remember what I said earlier about Gillette, with its enduring inventions, or Procter & Gamble, with its long-term success of Tide detergent? Microsoft, the blockbuster software company, has created the Tide detergent of computers: the DOS operating system that has become the standard of the IBM-compatible computer industry. We've liked Microsoft from time to time, when the price is right.

Avoid the fads. Stick to what sticks around.

And if you're thinking of investing in the company that makes the Slinky, don't bother. It's a private company in Hollidaysberg, Pennsylvania, owned by a woman who, so far, has resisted every offer to sell out.

AIRLINES OR BEDSPRINGS?

If the airlines would let me stand up and grab onto a handrail—like I would on a bus—I'd do it, as long as they let me fly cheaper. I'm not a big fan of the airlines, and I certainly don't need all the trappings of air flight today. At least, not for the cost of a round-trip ticket, anyway. I wonder whether the airlines would be more profitable if they'd let me fly my way and dispense with the elaborate meals, the wine list and the telephone in every seat.

I've been told that in the aggregate, the entire airline industry has lost money in the 90-odd years since the Wright brothers invented heavier-than-air flight. The combined balance sheet for every airline in the world is bleeding with red ink. I'm inclined to believe it after seeing so many Florida-based airlines bite the dust, including Florida Air and the two majors, Pan Am and Eastern.

With that kind of record, I wonder why anyone would want to invest in an airline. They are volatile and unreliable. And, obviously, there are exceptions: Southwest Air has shown it can be profitable for years and years (and they don't have all the trappings of air travel today). That's the sort of story that keeps airline investors going, I suppose.

The point: As an investor, you need to define your risk very carefully before you drop a penny into your brokerage account. If you don't mind some risk, some volatility with the chance of large short-term gains, maybe airlines are a good place to put your chips. Many people—including me—aren't interested in *that* much risk with little visible reward.

Of course, there's nowhere you can put your money—not even under the mattress—that is completely free of risk. If a burglar doesn't steal the cash out from under your bedsprings, inflation will sap it of its buying power. A certificate of deposit. . . . Well, we've been through that already. You're risking time, if not money.

The question is not *whether* to risk your money, but how *much* risk you can stomach.

SHORT TAKES

Do your homework. Pick the industries you like and the companies within those industries that look exciting. Learn as much as you can about those companies, so when something happens—good or bad—you're ready to react. When a trader calls me with 850,000 shares of Air Products for sale, I'd better be ready to make a decision right then. That block won't be around for long. I know the company, I know where its stock routinely trades, I know its value relative to the market. I've done all that work already. Now, I just need to decide: yes or no? And if I haven't done my homework, then I just say no!

Wait till you have ideas. Although I have strongly recommended that you should be fully invested in the stock market all the time, that doesn't mean you should throw money into the market when you don't like what's out there. Don't feel compelled to spend your cash if you don't have any good stock ideas right now. Hang on while you're looking. Better to spend the cash on good ideas than throw it at mediocre ones. Just don't waste a lot of time when opportunity knocks.

Make a checklist. I've said it before. I do it myself. You've seen me refer to the stock recommendations folks in my office write about hundreds of companies. As far as I'm concerned, those are checklists. What does this company do? What's the price now? What's its range? How does its p/e ratio compare to the market's and what are the projections? What is happening now that makes this company look like an attractive investment? Check back every once in a while to see if those reasons are still valid (and if the projections are still good). If so, hang on. If not, sell.

Make your own decisions. Nobody can tell you when to sell your stock. Don't rely on anyone else. It is usually not in anybody's interest to bad-mouth a stock, and if you're waiting for someone—a broker, a magazine article, anybody—to tell you to sell, then don't bother. You'll be waiting a long time. Besides, even if someone does tell you to sell, then they're usually basing it on information that's old and tired. By the time you get the word, it will have been acted upon a thousand times already. Here's another way to say it: You must anticipate good or bad news rather than reacting to it after it happens.

With Procter & Gamble in early 1993, when "consumer" stocks were out of favor (with me and a lot of investors), I didn't need to think twice when someone offered it for sale at $45 a share—a sharp decline from where it had recently sold. The company was sound and the price was cheap, so I was buying. When it climbed back to $56 eight months later, I was selling.

Develop your own discipline for buying and selling.

Don't time the market. You'll fail. Most everyone else does. Why should you be any different?

18

The Seven Deadly Sins

Throughout this book, I've told you stories about investments I've made—some that were brilliant stock plays from the start, others that started out well and soured, some that should never have happened in the first place. We've talked about the mistakes investors can make when they don't buckle down and pay attention or when they don't bother to invest in the first place. At the very start of the book, I alluded to the "seven deadly sins" of investing, but I've never really put them together until now. You will recognize some of these stories; we've discussed them before in other contexts. A few will be new. The idea, however, is to get you thinking about why you're investing, what your goals are and what to avoid when you call up your broker and open your portfolio account for the first time.

You'll also see, for example, that there's a fine line between being overconfident (one of the sins) and being timid or fearful. Take one step in one direction and you're missing an opportunity; one step in another direction and you're bold and forceful in your investment decisions. Take still one more step and you're all bluster

219

and boast, creating unrealistic expectations for your stocks and for yourself.

So there, I've spilled the beans on two of the sins already. The others: Don't be impatient, ignorant, dumb (there's a difference), disillusioned or stubborn. Trying to think of a clever way to remember all these sins—isn't that what these books are supposed to do?—I took the first letters for all seven sins and scrambled them around. The best I could come up with was "ID-DIOTS," which somehow doesn't seem like the tone we're going for in this chapter. So let's skip the clever memory techniques and move on.

DON'T BE DUMB

This is a tough rule to follow. Believe me, I know. I've broken it more than a few times. But I've had plenty of opportunities to capitalize on the dumb moves of others. Buying CPC International in the midst of a stock market crash, a story I've told you before, is just one example.

Another came in December 1993, when a trader offered a large chunk of Mobil Oil stock for sale. Frankly, we had soured a bit on energy stocks at the time—not that I ever really liked them. My colleagues and I felt oil prices were going down, and most people were getting out of those kinds of stocks. At the same time, we couldn't figure out whether there was any more bad news coming out. Let's face it: Everyone knew oil prices were going down. No surprise there. So suddenly, a very large block of Mobil comes on the market.

The market price was $77. I bid $74. Absurd. I didn't really want the stock that bad, so why not? Meanwhile, as I said, I didn't see anything wrong with Mobil Oil that everyone on earth didn't already know. The funny thing is, the seller bit. He sold the stock for the price we offered. We created a new market price for Mobil and guess what? The price never dropped lower than that, and it not only rose again right away, but also continued to rise for several days after that. We sold the stock again 10 days later for $80 a share.

I don't like energy stocks, and I don't know very much about them. But I would rather buy them when they are off 20 percent than when they're up 20 percent. How's that for a sophisticated philosophy?

Who knows why the Mobil story happened? Maybe the seller had too much energy and felt like he needed to get rid of some of it. Or maybe he was just dumb. After all, he left about four points on the table in that trade—money that could have been in his pocket instead of mine. I wouldn't have bought the stock if I didn't think it was a dumb thing for him to do.

He panicked. He knew everything I knew about the stock market and the economy and the company in question, but he decided everything spelled calamity. For the life of me, I don't know why.

Of course, I'm not immune to bouts of dumbness. I'm capable of supreme feats of it, in fact, and I do it often enough to keep me humble.

Remember Kinder-Care? It seemed like a good idea at the time—and for a while, it was a good idea. I couldn't buy the stock fast enough. I was even bold and ambitious as the stock price fell from $12 to $9 and further. That's what I've told you to do, right? When the stock price falls and you still like the story of the stock, grab your bushel basket and buy as fast as you can, right?

Well, in this case, the story changed. I watched the story change before my eyes, and I stood there and did nothing about it. I watched the management of Kinder-Care invest in banks, savings and loans and insurance companies, diversifying into companies that had nothing to do with the business of caring for children. I violated my own cardinal rule for investing: Know why you're buying a stock, know why you're holding a stock and make sure all those reasons are in place from time to time. It was only pure luck that I didn't lose more money than I did in Kinder-Care. I think I learned my lesson on that one.

Now, I'll grant you: Determining who is dumb isn't always that easy to do. There is also a fine line between dumb and smart, sometimes. There are ups and downs in the stock market every day. When somebody sells a stock that's down and I buy it, I look smart, right? But it is tough to determine in the short term whether the stock is down because it was a bad trade or because the seller knows something you don't know. The best you can do is ask whether the market is right or whether your story is right. And hope for the best when the dust settles.

DON'T BE IGNORANT

There is a difference between being *dumb* and being *ignorant*. I've done both, so I can assure you there is a difference. "Dumbness" is a sin of commission. You have the information, you know what you're supposed to be doing, yet you do the wrong thing anyway. Ignorance is a sin of omission. You weren't paying attention that day; you don't have the right information because it wasn't available, or you couldn't find it or you didn't even know you were supposed to look for it. And for that, you pay.

That's how it was for the farmer and businessman in the brokerage during lunch hour. Each was ignorant of the other's world— so ignorant, they didn't know enough about how to play stocks or commodities correctly. Yet they were quite savvy about their own worlds, savvy enough to know that they weren't prepared to invest their money that way.

That is also how it was for me as a novice investor in the early 1960s, when I bought United Fruit and watched it rise without understanding a single reason for it. The reason it later plummetted to half its price was obvious: Fidel Castro had taken control of the banana plantations. You didn't have to be an economics professor or a Harvard MBA to figure that out. But again, when the stock started to rise, I didn't know why. In fact, I still don't.

It was the same thing with Philip Morris. I overstayed a good thing with that stock. It had served me well for many, many years. I had seen earnings grow 20 percent a year, I had watched the dividends yield 3 percent to 5 percent a year in addition to growth in the stock price. And I maintained a constant vigil on the news of the day. It didn't even occur to me to watch the price of cigarettes and the changing market of consumers, who started demanding cut-rate cigarettes instead of the Marlboro Man. Of course, the hot-shot Wall Street analysts (who are supposed to focus on tobacco companies for a living) missed it too.

This goes back to my cardinal rule: You can't invest intelligently if you don't know why your stocks are going up and down. We all *expect* our stocks to rise when we buy them. Presumably, we even know the reason *why* they're rising if that expectation is correct. But if the stock falls, we also have to figure out why. The reason may not be fatal; we may want to buy even more of the stock as the price falls—but you won't know unless you have all the information.

DON'T BE TIMID

The one thing you can't do in investments is lose your nerve.

Of course, you can commit this sin even if you never had any nerve in the first place. For people who have money to spend, this can be a deadly sin before they ever sink a cent into the stock market because they are too afraid of Wall Street to give it a try. They're sticking close to home, stuffing their cash into long-term certificates of deposit as if they were some sort of magical cookie jar in their kitchen. Meanwhile, they're watching deflation kill the interest rate on their CDs, slashing their income into ribbons. Or they're watching inflation gobble up the buying power of that income before they have a chance to withdraw their investment and move it into something more lucrative. Frankly, this is probably the worst sin of the bunch.

But even if you dove into the stock market with both feet, you can still blow it by being a timid investor. When an opportunity arises to do something big, you have to be ready to grab it. You must have done your homework (or, to use my old analogy, you have to know what you already have in your closet so you're ready to buy when you find a new suit on sale). I'll give you a couple of examples.

Very early in this book, you read about my investment in International Game Technology, the makers of fine gambling devices everywhere. How did it do?

In a word: awful. In the last quarter of 1993, it tumbled from $40 a share to $28, and we owned about 200,000 shares worth. It dropped further and further, but we couldn't figure out why. Knowing what I know about the stock market, I listened carefully. Something must be wrong, the market was telling me. We kept checking and doing our research, and we couldn't find the problem. No negative stories about International Game.

In fact, everything was great. So I decided the market must be wrong.

And we bought more. The more the stock fell, the more we bought. By the end of our buying streak, we had accumulated another 300,000 shares, each share purchased a few cents cheaper than the share before it. The average cost of those additional 300,000 shares came to $29.50. By the end of the year, the stock had started to rally again. I think the stock will double by 1996. Don't forget to check the newspaper in a few years and see how I did. I don't see any reason to worry right now.

You must be ready to act when a buying opportunity comes along. I mentioned Air Products earlier in the book too, but I didn't discuss that trade in much detail. The fact is, there wasn't much to say the day I bought it. As you may recall, a trader called me late one morning with almost one million shares of the stock for sale. The market price was $44 a share; the seller wanted $41.50 for it. A deal like that doesn't sit around forever. When something like that comes around, you need to be ready to make a decision. In June 1993, I bought 845,000 shares for the discounted price, figuring I had made a great play.

As it turned out, neither the seller nor I looked very good for a while there. For five months, the stock didn't work, selling at or slightly below the price I'd paid for it. But I didn't have any reason to dump the stock. The fundamentals of the company were getting stronger, earnings were improving and the economy was getting better—something that could only help Air Products, a cyclical company that supplies industrial gases such as oxygen and nitrogen. People will eat the same amount of Cheerios whether times are good or bad; industry won't buy as much compressed nitrogen for its products if times are bad, however.

Well, apparently I was finally right and the seller was wrong. I was just a little early. By the beginning of 1994, the stock was performing great. The price had rallied to $49 a share ($7.50 more than I paid for it). At that price, I sold some of it and bought it back a few weeks later for $46.50. In fact, as I write this, I'm expecting the stock to hit $55 sometime this year.

The story is similar with Fruit of the Loom. A few years earlier, in 1990, I had started buying Fruit when it sold for nearly $12.00 a share. Then the stock started slipping lower and lower. A few months later, it dipped all the way down to $6.50 a share, about half what I'd first paid for it. All the while, I was buying up the stock. I liked Fruit of the Loom, I thought the story was good. The only difference: The main shareholder and CEO of the company had personal financial problems. For the market, it was a psychological blow. Would the owner's personal finances drag down the stock? I didn't think so. Turns out I was right. By the time my Procter & Gamble deal rolled around, Fruit was selling for $21 a share. The other problems with Fruit of the Loom (that we discussed earlier) didn't come along till later. This time around, I had my story and I stuck to it. This time, I felt the market was wrong, I was willing to put my money where my mouth was and I was right.

To invest in the stock market is automatically a sign of boldness. The timid fail immediately. The simple act of buying a stock is a bold announcement: My perception of this stock is right and everyone else (who didn't buy it) is wrong. It's too easy to talk yourself out of doing anything because nobody wants to look dumb. The stock market, like any other investment, has its share of risk. There is always the *chance* that one or two (or more!) of your investment decisions will be losers. In fact, the chances are extremely good that you'll make many mistakes; everybody does. But if you let fear of that risk paralyze you, you don't have a chance. You're doomed from the start.

DON'T BE OVERCONFIDENT

Just a stone's throw away from timidness is overconfidence. I make an investment decision. It was right. Aren't I great? Suddenly, you're feeling infallible, spouting off about your great ideas. You might even catch yourself starting sentences with, "And now, for my next trick...."

It happened to me with Waste Management, the world's largest trash hauler. Somehow, even when things seemed to sour, I thought I knew the score and kept believing in the stock.

Waste Management started in 1971. It was the product of a corporate marriage between an Illinois trash hauler who started with 12 trucks and a Florida trash hauler who started with two. Now, it has become a $7.6 billion business. We started investing in Waste Management when it was just a baby, only 11 years old, in 1982.

To digress for just a moment, this is another classic example of how my investment philosophy works. We didn't just buy Waste Management; we swapped between Waste and Browning-Ferris, one of its largest competitors. We would compare both companies' p/e ratios with the market's, determine which one looked cheaper and buy it. Remember: The cheaper stock is the one with the most potential upside, the one whose price can grow the most.

In the early 1980s, we would expect Waste Management to trade constantly at a premium to the market, between 140 percent and 180 percent of the market's p/e ratio. Browning-Ferris would maintain a slightly lower range. From time to time, we'd have stock recommendations sheets that read like this: "Waste is off 22 percent since our March 18, 1988, sell recommendation, while Browning-Ferris is up 17 percent. This is due to a number of allegations by some former (Waste) employees and state officials concerning illegal disposal techniques. All of these have been dealt with by Waste with little cost to the company or any appearance of wrongdoing. You can now buy Waste; before this flap, it sold at a substantial premium to Browning-Ferris."

Back and forth we'd go, selling Waste when it got ahead of Browning-Ferris and vice versa. In February 1986, when both think so, apparently. The trader hung up to consult with his client and called back with the client's counteroffer: $35.12 a share, $.13 *cheaper* than the market price. I guess he thought he would be doing me a favor if he relieved me of 200,000 shares of GM. I laughed and offered another price, $35.75 a share, higher than my last offer. I knew what would happen. The trader disappeared, and I didn't hear from him again.

I had a point to make. I wanted the trader (and his client) to know that bidding $35.12 was just plain absurd. He forgot who was on the other end of the phone. So who was being stubborn?

In my view, he was. I didn't want the stock, but I sure didn't want to *give* it away. Maybe he knew something I didn't know. Maybe his story on GM was better than mine. There must have been some reason he wanted to buy 200,000 shares of it at the time. Unfortunately, he wanted to steal it, not buy it. I guess I can't blame him. I try to do the same thing!

It's easy to find stubborn investors in the stock market. They buy a stock and hang on to it forever, expecting it to keep rising and rising and rising. I don't subscribe to that notion. I trade. I buy the stocks that look as though they have room to rise because they're selling cheap. To make the real money, you must trade. If you always think your stock is going higher, then that's being stubborn.

That doesn't mean I recommend you have the sort of turnover I have in my portfolio. Everything I own gets sold about once during a year's time. I have at least 100 percent turnover, too high for the individual who isn't paying strict attention to his holdings at all times.

That also doesn't mean I never hold a stock for a long time. It just depends on the price, whether or not it's cheap. I have owned stock in General Electric for 12 years. There was nothing magic about it; I just never felt the stock sold for the price it should have. I always thought it looked cheap.

There's another sign of stubborness that we've discussed before. Look for those investors who had a bad idea and lost a lot of money on it. Instead of admitting they made a mistake and moving on, they dig their heels into the dirt. As the stock drags them down companies posted an identical p/e of 19.5 (and both sold at a 50 percent premium to the market), we issued this recommendation: "Waste has earned and *should* earn at much better growth rates than Browning. They should *not* sell at the same p/e. SWITCH!"

This continued throughout the decade as Waste's stock price basically shot straight up to around $60 a share by 1990 when it reached its peak. We felt that the company's earnings would slow during the recession at the time, but it would come back. We had no reason to think otherwise; the company had done nothing but grow, grow, grow for 10 years. For the first year of the recession, we were right. Sales and earnings did hold up. So what's the logical conclusion if you figure you've been right about everything else up to now? Sure: Keep buying Waste Management. If it did fine *during* the recessions, then it should do great as the recession ends.

While I was waiting for Waste Management to boom, the recession ended, and the company's stock fell from $45 a share to $30. We had been listening to the wrong analysts, who were telling us what we wanted to hear. And I had a slice of humble pie.

When you're an overconfident investor, you start feeling like you're a little bit infallible. But the best investors are only right between 50 percent and 55 percent of the time. That hardly classifies anyone as infallible.

DON'T BE STUBBORN

The Waste Management story has elements of this sin in it as well. I see it all the time. People get ideas in their heads and they won't budge. I saw it in late 1991 when a trader called offering to buy 200,000 shares of General Motors. Great! I thought. GM is a dog. I hated the stock at the time and was waiting for a chance to get rid of some it. My opportunity had come in through the phone line.

I am, of course, not going to let the stock sail out of my portfolio without doing a little bargaining. That's just not my style. I offered to sell the stock for $35.62 a share, $.12 higher than the market price at the time. A reasonable offer for such a large trade. He didn't further and further, you can see the fresh furrows plowed up by those stubborn heels. Or you can see those investors sinking in the mud as the stock stagnates, doing nothing for months and months. Those folks are waiting until the stock returns to their purchase price so they can get their money back. Meanwhile, as they stubbornly await a miracle, they are missing the chance to invest in new ideas and make back the money somewhere else.

Don't Be Impatient

It's amazing how often these sins overlap. In fact, it's probably impossible to commit one without committing several of them at the same time. I wonder if it's possible to commit all seven at once?

Stubborn investors can easily be impatient as well. You can buy Fruit of the Loom at $12 and watch it tumble but assume your story is wrong instead of the stock market. You sell and miss a chance to watch it run to $50 when the market comes to its senses. You weren't patient. You might conclude that because I have a high level of turnover in my portfolio, I'm not patient. Not so. You just need to know when patience will be rewarded.

You can also see how these sins can sometimes be mirror images of each other. For example, the impatient investor hears bad news about a stock and sells immediately, before taking time to assess the damage and deciding whether it's really bad news or just a fluke. The stubborn investor hears more and more bad news, assumes there is nothing to worry about and hangs on until things turn around instead of admitting a mistake, selling out and moving on. The stubborn investor can also be wrong when a stock is ready to climb: Some good news comes out about ABC Widget, but the stubborn investor wants to see more (maybe he or she is from Missouri?). A little more positive news trickles out and pretty soon, the stubborn investor missed the ride. The stock has come up as other investors *anticipate* more good news. Meanwhile, the stubborn investor is still saying, "Show me"—or "Show me more!"

Another symptom of impatient investors: They want to see their money grow *now*. They don't let that magical concept work for them:

compound interest. They're not content to see a stock rise a little now, a little later and then see the results in a few years. They want 10 percent or 20 percent returns instantly. That might have been conceivable in the 1980s, when the economy was performing like a thoroughbred race horse, but it's not likely to happen in the years to come.

DON'T BE DISILLUSIONED

I've mentioned this mistake before. Mr. Investor buys a stock and it goes down. He has had a bad experience in the stock market. Forevermore, he shies from stocks like a horse from a snake. Don't make that mistake. For heaven's sake, if you take nothing away from this book, remember this: *Every investor on the planet makes mistakes about half the time.* The successful investors limit their mistakes to 45 percent of the time. But putting your money on the line in the market means you have to be willing to take your lumps sometimes.

That doesn't mean you hang on to a stock forever; we've been through that before already. It means you hang on to your investments as a whole. Don't pull out all your money so you can buy a new car. Develop and maintain an investment strategy—your style. Stick with it. Even if there is a Crash of 2000, don't pull all your money out of the stock market and assume life as we know it is over. Chances are, you'd probably put your money *back* in the stock market two years later, after the market rallied 50 percent, missing your chance to profit and recoup your losses from the crash.

People tend to get interested in the stock market when it's strong and lose interest again when it's not. That's one version of a market timer. If you jump in and out, changing your investment style every time the economic cycles change, you're wasting your time and fattening your broker's wallet as he rakes in commissions from your wasted trades.

Go forth, and sin no more.

19

A Final Q & A

We're winding down to the end now. In the speeches I give to investors, I spend about a half hour talking off the top of my head about the stock market, my investments, what I like and don't like. I spend a little time telling people what I think they might like or want to know.

Then I open the floor for questions. Unfortunately, I can't see any of your raised hands out there right now, so the best I can do is try to answer some of the questions I know I get asked a lot. So, without further ado, are there any questions out there?

HOW DO YOU DECIDE WHICH STOCKS TO FOLLOW AND WHICH TO BUY?

You follow several stocks in several industry types. Look for a stock that tends to have positive characteristics that you like. If you're a growth stock investor, then you want something that has a good growth story like a Wal-Mart or a Home Depot. If you're an income investor, you want something with a safe dividend that increases modestly, but regularly—maybe an energy stock or a long-distance telephone company. You need a story that is fairly simple; one that someone can tell and explain the merits to you in a short time.

After a half hour, if you still can't understand the stock, then you probably ought to move on to the next one. In my case, growth stocks, I look for a company that has grown well, that has a product which is in demand and better than any other company's products, and that I can see growing in absolute terms, where the profitability of whatever it's selling is good and improving.

When and why do you sell a stock?

First, list the reasons why you want to buy a stock. If you're talking about a growth stock, you say, "Well, I like it because it has good products, and the company has been growing 20 percent to 30 percent a year. We think it can continue at that rate, and it is cheap relative to some benchmark" such as the market as a whole or other growth stocks, other companies in the industry. We'd sell it when it no longer met those criteria. Let's say the company had a great product, and the product has become obsolete or someone has a better one. Or it's been growing at a slower growth rate—a lot slower. Management changes, a competitor comes along.

My favorite reason to sell is I bought a stock when it was cheap, and it's gone up in value, and I don't think it's cheap anymore.

Should i consider the international markets?

I am not much of an international investor; not because I don't believe in it, but because I don't have a lot of skill in it. If you think investing in the American markets is tough, then you ought to try the international markets. You may think that a hamburger will sell well in this country, but a foreign country may not have any interest in it at all. A certain retailing concept might be great in this country but not work at all in a foreign country. Breakfast cereal is a great item here. Americans eat a lot of it. But in other countries, they may not eat breakfast at all, let alone breakfast cereal. So there's a lot of things to consider.

No doubt there are emerging markets of the world—Mexico, Latin America, China, the Asian areas, for example. If you have some skills and pick the right times and the right companies, then these will be good areas to invest in. There are a lot of mature markets of the world where I don't see that kind of growth. The United States is certainly a very mature market with an aging population. Europe is an even more mature market with an even older population. Japan I think has seen its growth days. It has a very old population.

DOES THE SIZE OF YOUR FUND HINDER ITS PERFORMANCE?

Yes. It is much easier to run $100 million than $1 billion. It's easier to run $1 billion dollars than $10 billion. The bigger you are the harder it gets. You lose the ability to be nimble in the market. It's one thing to own 50,000 shares of a stock. If you own 2 million shares of it and then there's a problem and you want to sell, who will buy that much of it?

WHAT DO YOU THINK OF THE MARKET?

Of course the market is overpriced or underpriced or properly priced. But we don't always know which one it is. An awful lot of people have sold out of stocks thinking the stocks were overpriced and they would buy them back at cheaper levels when the market corrects. They never get back in the market. Or they don't go back in when the market corrects because then they are thinking the market will go down even more.

I tend to stay almost fully invested all the time because there are a lot of times that I think the market is overpriced and I can raise some cash and I turn out to be wrong. I think the market is a place to make money, I think I will make more money than the next guy will, so why do I want to be out of the market with very much money or for very long?

WHY DID GROWTH STOCKS AND HIGHLY RATED STOCKS PERFORM POORLY IN 1992-93 (E.G., MERCK, BIG RETAILERS LIKE THE HOME DEPOT, WAL-MART, PACKAGED FOODS?)

Growth stocks did extremely well in the 1980s, but in the early 1990s the growth rates started to slip for most of these—health care stocks, primarily, but even Wal-Mart. There are cycles in the market where people like growth stocks, they like big growth stocks, they like small growth stocks, they like value stocks and they like income stocks. It's great if you can anticipate these changes, but most of the time you can't. So if your style is out of favor, you make some adjustments, but primarily, you just have to live with it.

SHOULD I FOCUS MONEY ON LONG-TERM CAPITAL GAINS, TAXABLE AT 28 PERCENT, OR SHOULD I BUY MUNICIPAL BONDS, WHICH GET PROTECTION AGAINST TAXES?

My feeling: In almost any environment, growth tends be a better vehicle. I'll keep my money in growth stocks.

IF A CD IS GETTING 3.1 PERCENT, DO YOU HAVE ANY STOCKS THAT ARE SAFE AND GET A BETTER YIELD?

You have to realize that nothing is perfectly safe. In a CD, your principal is safe. If you give the bank $100,000, you can get it back. It's the same with a government bill. At maturity, you get that back.

But what you're not protected from is what happened in the early 1980s when inflation was running rampant. Though you might have a high-quality long-term bond, you might have bought it at 100, and it might have gone down to 60 because inflation ate into the market value of the bond. So that was not safe. The CD you bought in the late 1980s at a 7 percent yield was down to 3 percent when you rolled it over in 1992; it was safe, but the reinvestment rate was not safe.

When CD rates surged again in late 1994, I still say you were wasting your time with them because they are short-term places to put money. In the long term, the stock market is always going to beat a CD.

Obviously, you can't ignore rising interest rates; heaven knows, the stock market doesn't. Higher interest rates are bad for the market primarily because they make other investment options look attractive. When interest rates rose in late 1994, I bought my first bond in three and a half years, but I didn't abandon the stock market. That's part of having a balanced portfolio, which is where the safety is found.

You buy stocks, we all know there is risk involved in that. Certainly each individual stock has a risk that is really hard to quantify. You know large financially strong companies have less risk than small emerging ones, but that doesn't protect them. You've seen major declines in the value and the fortunes of what were formerly strong growth stocks like Kmart. Safety only comes with diversification. If you have a bond portfolio, then you need to diversify the maturities and the qualities. In stocks, you need to diversify into different industries. That is the way I would get safe. The risk in a diversified portfolio is far less than the risk in any one of those stocks.

If you want yield right now, you used to look at electric utilities. That's not an area I like; I don't think there is any growth in electric utilities, so I wouldn't do that. You can invest in an income mutual fund that invests in higher yielding stocks, and you can get a 4 percent yield that way. There is a fair amount of safety in that.

YOU ARE KNOWN AS A GROWTH STOCK INVESTOR BUT GROWTH SUCH AS IN DRUGS, FOOD COMPANIES AND THE LIKE DOESN'T SEEM TO BE WORKING. WHAT ARE YOU DOING NOW?

Well there's growth and there's growth. We went through the 1980s and all the same stocks were the growers. If an area stops growing, then you get out of that area, and you look for new areas that are growing. There are always new areas that are growing that weren't around a few years ago or that weren't around in sufficient size to justify your investments. That's what I have done. I have not sold Merck and bought Caterpillar (although that would have been a pretty good thing to do). But I have sold drug stocks and bought HMOs, sold companies that make branded products and bought companies selling store brands—Cott, for instance, which we discussed earlier, or Perrigo would be examples of those. Perrigo makes store brand products such as aspirin and toothpaste. If you've ever seen a bottle of Head & Shoulders shampoo sitting next to an identical bottle of a store brand dandruff shampoo, you've probably seen a Perrigo product.

How do you know when cyclical stocks have had their final run?

You don't. That's why it's so hard to play cyclical stocks. You don't know when the cycle is going to start, and you don't know when it's going to end. The stocks will stop performing and will roll over and start going down a fair amount before the fundamentals will. If you're playing autos and you think they'll do well until 1997, then you'll probably want to start getting out around 1996 and give yourself at least a year ahead to do it. Nobody rings a bell to tell you when to sell. When earnings are dropping, profit margins are under pressure, pricing is under pressure, you need to have already sold.

How do you know when to give up the ghost, when the individual security is doing poorly, and you want to take your losses and run?

When to sell is one of the most difficult questions to answer. Look at the reasons you bought the stock in the first place. If those reasons aren't there, then that might be a reason to sell. But what happens when you bought it at $50 and now it's at $25, and it seems there is a lot of disappointment with the stock? Well, you have to step away, take a candid view and forget about the fact that you paid $50 for it.

The market doesn't know and doesn't care what you paid for it. You have to say it's now at $25, it's going to earn this, its position is this—basically, you have to evaluate it all over again. A good question to ask yourself is this: If I didn't own it, would I buy it? If the answer is no, then you probably ought to sell it or at least sell some of it. On the other hand, if the answer is yes, you probably ought to hold onto your stock—or buy more.

How can the inflation rate be 3 percent when everything costs me more?

The answer is that you're only paying attention to the things that are costing you more. Look at the things that are not going up. Look at the the things that are going down, and there are a lot of them. Housing, for example. In 1988, if you wanted to buy $150,000 house, you financed it at 9 percent, and you had a pretty substantial mortgage payment. Now you could buy that house for 10 percent less, and your interest rate is 7 percent. In April 1993, a pack of cigarettes was cut substantially. Look at that home computer you bought; you might have paid $1,500. Five years ago, you couldn't have bought anything with that kind of money. You wouldn't buy a semiconductor chip, but trust me: They're far cheaper and far more powerful than they used to be. A couple of years ago, McDonald's cut the price of hamburgers. Taco Bell cut the price of tacos. That's deflation. Take gasoline. It's under a dollar in some places. It went over a dollar in 1974; it was over that subtantially in 1981–82. You have to look at the things that are *not* going up or that are even going down.

Can a bond fund lose money?

It most certainly can. They have lost money a lot of times. Let's say you buy a 30-year bond that yields 6.5 percent. What happens if interest rates go to 7.5 percent? This bond is going to go down into the 80s. You won't lose money if you keep it for 30 years, but there are very few people who make an investment and don't change it for 30 years. Bond funds are not guaranteed by anybody.

WHAT CAUSES INTEREST RATES TO RISE?

Generally, better economic times cause rates to rise. It's a function of inflation and expectations for inflation. If the economy gets strong, if there is more demand for copper, for example, and it goes from $.80 a pound to $1.10 a pound, that's inflation. That would cause a lot of things to go up. The federal reserve board, if it feels the economy is growing too rapidly, will arbitrarily increase interest rates to keep the economy at a more moderate pace.

HOW SAFE ARE STOCK DIVIDENDS?

You have to look at each company. If a company is earning $5 and paying out $2 in dividends, you have to assume it's safe, at least for a while. Take IBM, which has cut its dividend substantially in the last several years. You could see it coming. Their earnings kept coming down, every quarter, every year lower than the one before. Pretty soon, they were paying out more dividends than they were earning.

Well you can't do that for very long. They had to cut the dividend. In fact, maybe they shouldn't be paying a dividend at all. If you pick your stocks carefully, then you should have a number of them that will be increasing their dividends, and this will help offset those that might get cut.

SHOULD I TRY TO ACTIVELY TRADE MY PORTFOLIO?

That depends on your skills. You have to have knowledge, you have to have skills, you have to pay attention to it. I trade very actively. But if you are not paying attention to it and you don't have any skill at this, then I wouldn't recommend trading too actively—especially as actively as me. I turn over my portfolio more than 100 percent a year. Just remember: The only time you realize any of the gains your stocks have made is when you sell them.

Should I choose an arbitrary number as a guide to buying or selling, say, sell if my stock drops by 15 percent?

I don't do that. If your stock goes down or up, you need to reevaluate it as if you didn't own it and say, "Would I buy it again?" If it has declined, why? A lot of stocks go down and there's no reason. I don't have a hard, fast rule to arbitrarily sell a stock.

Why do stocks generally go up in January?

There are a number of January effects. The market tends to go up; small stocks tend to do better; cyclicals do better. What is the reason? There's a lot of money that comes into the market in January. Pension funds put in new allocations, people get bonuses. If they put money in the market, there are more buyers than sellers, therefore it's going to go up. Small stocks do well in January just because people are more optimistic. Certainly with cyclicals, you come off the previous year and earnings were off in the last quarter, for some reason, people associate the new year with renewed optimism. They pump money in and slowly, slowly drift away as the year winds down—if nothing good has happened to their stock.

How much do you think the market could go up?

I haven't any idea. Over the long term the market goes up. For the last few years my feeling has been that the market would have more modest gains than it did during the 1980s. That's generally been the case. In 1993, the market was up about 10 percent, a similar number the previous year. But we've watched it go up almost non-stop since 1982. These days, everyone thinks the market always goes up. Of course, that's not the case.

On the 16th anniversary of my getting into the business in 1982, the market was priced lower than it was in 1966. So I felt like I deserved the last 11 years of gains. It was very difficult before that.

There were a lot of reasons—primarily inflation and a number of recessions—why all this happened. Certainly the market goes down. Would it surprise me if, when you're reading this, the market goes down 10 percent? Absolutely not. I would say it's long overdue, but that shouldn't dissuade you from owning stocks. A market drop of 10 percent or 15 percent is common.

WILL THE MARKET HAVE ANOTHER CRASH?

It should have another correction. An 8 percent or 10 percent correction is extremely common. A 15 percent one is not that unusual. The 20 percent or 25 percent ones are the big ones. But I'm not predicting a crash. I didn't predict the last one, so why should I predict the next one?

WHERE DO YOU THINK INTEREST RATES ARE HEADING?

We had a rule in our shop that we were not allowed to predict interest rates because the past has shown that we're not very good at it. I think it's a difficult thing to do. The 5.8 percent long-term treasury rate is the lowest it will reach. So I think it will be higher. Do I think these rates will reach 9 percent? That's probably the upper limit. I think inflation is under control. I would look in 1995 and 1996 for long-term government rates to be in the 6.5 percent to 8 percent range.

HOW HAS YOUR FUND DONE IN BEAR MARKETS—THE MARKETS THAT AREN'T PERFORMING WELL?

Good question. While everyone wants to make a lot of money when the market is good, nobody wants to lose any money either when the market is not so good. You take it very personally. Any time the market is down and your fund is down, you'll have people say, "I could have done better in a CD." That may be true, but you don't know which year the market is going to go down. It will go down some time. I've been running this fund now since 1981 and I've never had a down year. Will I have a down year in the next five years? I'm sure I probably will.

What percentage of return would you guess your fund or the market will do over the next 1, 5 or 10 years?

We don't know. My goal is to beat the S&P 500 every year. I have done it 11 out of 13 years. I will say it seems to get harder every year as my fund gets bigger. I don't know whether the next years will be good or lean. I think it is somewhere between difficult and impossible to know. You get in there, you come to work every day, you do your investments, you buy and sell. If you work hard at it and you're skillful, at the end of that period, you do better than the person who didn't work hard and isn't as skillful. That's about all you can count on.

What do you think about putting money into real estate instead of stocks?

I have a real interest in real estate. I like to drive around and look at houses, see what things are worth, see the prices at which houses or real estate changes hands. The couple of times I've owned it (other than my home), I've found it very frustrating. You can't get your money when you want it. It's not liquid. It could take anywhere from 6 to 18 months to sell it—longer if it's an office building. In a low-inflation period, I don't think the returns are going to be high enough to warrant the extreme nuisance of investing in it.

When you buy a stock, you may or may not get a stock certificate. Either your broker keeps it or you put it in your safety deposit box. You never have to mow the lawn, you never have to wash the windows. It's a lot easier to own stocks. If you decide you don't want it anymore, you just have to sell it, and you get pretty much the price that's quoted in the paper—not so with real estate.

Do you own gold stocks?

No. I've never owned them. I think it's silly to contemplate owning gold. And the folks who own gold bars probably also own stock in companies that mine gold. I find it has no real merit other than for speculation. At least with copper, it has an economic value. There are people that are good at investing in gold, and I guess they make money in it. But remember in 1980, gold was over $800 and now it's $385. So you haven't missed anything. I wouldn't waste one iota of thought on whether to invest in gold.

DO YOU BUY ANY REALLY RISKY STOCKS?

A lot of times you don't know how risky the things are until you've bought them, and they didn't work out. But yes, I think there's a place for risky stocks if you know what you're doing and you buy significantly smaller positions than you would in a quality stock.

EPILOGUE

Imagine playing tennis with an army infantry backpack strapped to your shoulders. That's a little bit like the situation I'm in as a fund manager. More than 13 years have passed since I started running SunBank's Corporate Equity Fund, and in that time, it has grown in value from a few million to well over a billion dollars in assets. Therefore, I can't move as fast, figuratively speaking, with my investments. I'm not as nimble as I used to be. It becomes harder and harder to achieve record-breaking levels of success. That's okay. My goals still remain the same, modest as ever: I just want to beat the market every year.

From 1981, when I started managing this fund, until the end of 1993, I have met that goal every year but two. As 1994 draws to a close, I am pessimistic about meeting my goal this time. I'm am still pleased with my record: Since 1981, the Standard & Poor's 500 index has increased 467.2 percent; my fund has increased 1,001.1 percent. I'll take that record—to the bank.

Annual Percentage Change in My Fund and the Market Since 1981

Year	Corp. Equity	S&P 500
1981	11.7%	-5.3%
1982	29.1	21.5
1983	33.3	22.6
1984	15.4	6.3
1985	47.8	31.8
1986	32.0	18.7
1987	16.3	5.2
1988	13.1	16.6
1989	35.7	31.7
1990	0.9	-3.2
1991	38.5	30.4
1992	6.8	7.6
1993	10.5	10.1

Index